Oxford Children's Rhyming Dictionary

OXFORD

UNIVERSITY PRESS

OXFORD
UNIVERSITY PRESS

Great Clarendon Street, Oxford, OX2 6DP,
United Kingdom

Oxford University Press is a department of the
University of Oxford. It furthers the University's
objective of excellence in research, scholarship, and education
by publishing worldwide. Oxford is a registered trade
mark of Oxford University Press in the UK and in certain
other countries

Text © John Foster 2004

The moral rights of the author have been asserted

First published 2005
Second edition 2008
This edition 2014

British Library Cataloguing in Publication Data
Data available

ISBN: 978-0-19273558-4

10 9 8 7 6 5 4

Paper used in the production of this book is a natural,
recyclable product made from wood grown in sustainable
forests. The manufacturing process conforms to the
environmental regulations of the country of origin.

Printed in Malaysia by Vivar Printing Sdn Bhd

Acknowledgements:

Illustrations by Melanie Williamson and Rupert Van Wyck

Oxford Children's Rhyming Dictionary

OXFORD

UNIVERSITY PRESS

How to use this dictionary

You can use this dictionary to help you to find words that rhyme. When you want to find the rhymes for a particular word, the A to Z index on page 146 will help you to find the right page in the dictionary.

You can also use the dictionary to learn how to spell words that belong to the same rhyming family. You will find an index of rhyming sounds on page 143.

The alphabet

The key words in this dictionary are listed in alphabetical order.
There is an alphabet line down the side of each page to help you to find your way around the dictionary.

Key words

A key word is a word that you use very often. In this dictionary, the key words are in **bold**. You can look up a key word and find a list of other words that rhyme with it.

Rhyme family

A rhyme family is a family of words that end with the same rhyming sound and have the same spelling pattern.

Each key word belongs to a rhyme family. You will find the rhyming sound after the key word.

Example

key word   *rhyming sound*

hole   *-ole*

rhyme family

mole   pole   role   sole   stole   vole   whole

Sometimes there are several words from one rhyme family which rhyme with words from another rhyme family.

Example

-ole rhymes with *-oal*
coal   foal   goal

-ole also rhymes with some *-oll* words
poll   roll   scroll   stroll   troll

And sometimes there are words that rhyme with the key word but have a different spelling pattern.

Example

Other words that rhyme with *mole*
bowl   soul

5

Rhymes

There are lots of rhymes throughout the dictionary. You can use these as a starting point for rhymes of your own.

A jaguar from Zanzibar
Learned to play the bass guitar.
Now he's a famous movie star
And drives round in a racing car.

Indexes

The dictionary has two indexes. The A to Z index on page 146 lists every word in this dictionary. The key words are printed in bold type. This index will tell you the page where you will find the rhyming word you are looking for.

The Index of rhyming sounds on page 143 lists every rhyming sound in this dictionary. You can look up the sound that you want to make rhymes with and go straight to the key word in the main part of the book.

Activities

There is a 'Write your own poetry' section on page 130. This suggests things you can do to practise making up rhymes and writing rhyming poems.

These are the features of the dictionary:

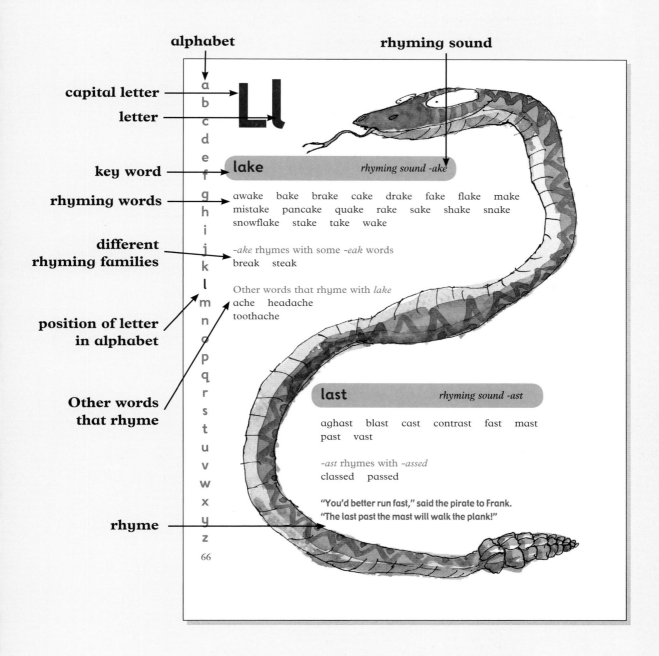

alphabet

rhyming sound

capital letter → Ll

letter

a b c d e f g h i j k l m n o p q r s t u v w x y z

key word → lake   *rhyming sound -ake*

rhyming words → awake bake brake cake drake fake flake make mistake pancake quake rake sake shake snake snowflake stake take wake

different rhyming families → *-ake* rhymes with some *-eak* words
break   steak

position of letter in alphabet

Other words that rhyme → Other words that rhyme with *lake*
ache   headache
toothache

last   *rhyming sound -ast*

aghast blast cast contrast fast mast
past vast

-ast rhymes with *-assed*
classed   passed

"You'd better run fast," said the pirate to Frank.
"The last past the mast will walk the plank!"

rhyme

66

7

Aa

act
rhyming sound -act

abstract attract compact contact contract distract
exact extract fact impact pact react subtract tact

-act rhymes with *-acked*
backed backpacked backtracked cracked hijacked
humpbacked lacked packed quacked sacked smacked
snacked stacked tracked unpacked whacked

air
rhyming sound -air

chair despair fair flair hair lair mid-air pair
repair stair unfair

-air rhymes with *-are*
aware bare beware blare care compare dare declare
fare glare hare mare nightmare prepare rare scare
share snare software spare square stare

-air rhymes with *-aire*
billionaire millionaire solitaire

Other words that rhyme with *air*
bear pear prayer swear their
there wear where

Ride on the Ghost Train if you dare.
Feel the spiders as they brush your hair.
Shiver at the gleaming eyes that stare.
Cringe as you pass the vampire's lair.

Ride on the Ghost Train **if you dare!**

a
b
c
d
e
f
g
h
i
j
k
l
m
n
o
p
q
r
s
t
u
v
w
x
y
z

9

ant   *rhyming sound -ant*

currant   descendant   elegant   elephant   pant
rant   scant

arm   *rhyming sound -arm*

alarm   charm   farm   harm

-arm rhymes with *-alm*
calm   palm

ask   *rhyming sound -ask*

bask   cask   flask   mask   task

Bb

bang   *rhyming sound -ang*

boomerang   clang   fang   gang   hang
overhang   pang   rang   sang   slang
sprang   tang   twang

As the midnight bell rang,
The werewolf bared its fang
And **sprang**.

bank *rhyming sound -ank*

blank   clank   crank   dank   drank   frank
lank   plank   prank   rank   sank   shrank
spank   stank   tank   thank   yank

beach *rhyming sound -each*

bleach   each   peach   preach   reach   teach

-each rhymes with *-eech*
beech   screech   speech

My sister gave a loud **screech**
As she bit through the slug in her peach.

a
b
c
d
e
f
g
h
i
j
k
l
m
n
o
p
q
r
s
t
u
v
w
x
y
z

belt *rhyming sound -elt*

celt   dwelt   felt   knelt   melt   pelt
spelt   welt

Another word that rhymes with *belt*
dealt

big *rhyming sound -ig*

dig   earwig   fig   gig   jig   oil rig   pig
rig   sprig   swig   twig   whirligig   wig

bike *rhyming sound -ike*

alike   dislike   hike   like   pike   spike   strike   trike

bird *rhyming sound -ird*

ladybird   third

Other words that rhyme with *bird*
absurd   blurred   heard   herd   nerd   preferred
purred   stirred   whirred   word

black *rhyming sound -ack*

attack   back   backpack   bareback   crack   flapjack
hack   haystack   horseback   jack   knack
lack   lumberjack   pack   piggyback
quack   rack   rucksack   sack
shack   slack   smack   snack
soundtrack   stack   tack
track   unpack   whack

Other words that rhyme
with *black*
anorak   kayak   mac   maniac
plaque   tarmac   yak

Mr Black, Mr Black,
Please can we have our
                football back?
You can pass it through
                the window.
It'll fit through the crack.
Oh, don't be a spoilsport, Mr Black.
Please give us our football back.

bone

rhyming sound -one

alone   clone   cone   drone   lone   megaphone   ozone   phone
postpone   prone   stone   timezone   throne   tombstone   tone
trombone   xylophone   zone

-one rhymes with *-own*
blown   flown   grown   known   own   shown   sown   thrown

Other words that rhyme with *bone*
groan   loan   moan   sewn

"I feel ill," said the king and gave a groan,
when he saw the bill for his mobile phone.

boot
rhyming sound -oot

b

beetroot   hoot   loot   reboot   root
scoot   shoot   toot

-oot rhymes with *-ute*

acute   brute   chute   cute   dilute   dispute   execute   flute
minute   mute   parachute   pollute   salute   substitute

Other words that rhyme with *boot*

fruit   newt   suit

An elephant in a parachute.

A koala bear playing the flute.

A penguin whizzing down a chute.

And a hippopotamus in a suit.

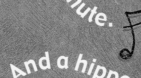
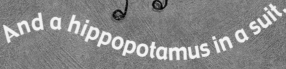

a
b
c
d
e
f
g
h
i
j
k
l
m
n
o
p
q
r
s
t
u
v
w
x
y
z

boss   *rhyming sound -oss*

across   albatross   candyfloss   cross   floss
gloss   loss   moss   toss

bounce   *rhyming sound -ounce*

announce   flounce   ounce   pounce
pronounce   trounce

bridge   *rhyming sound -idge*

fridge   midge
porridge   ridge

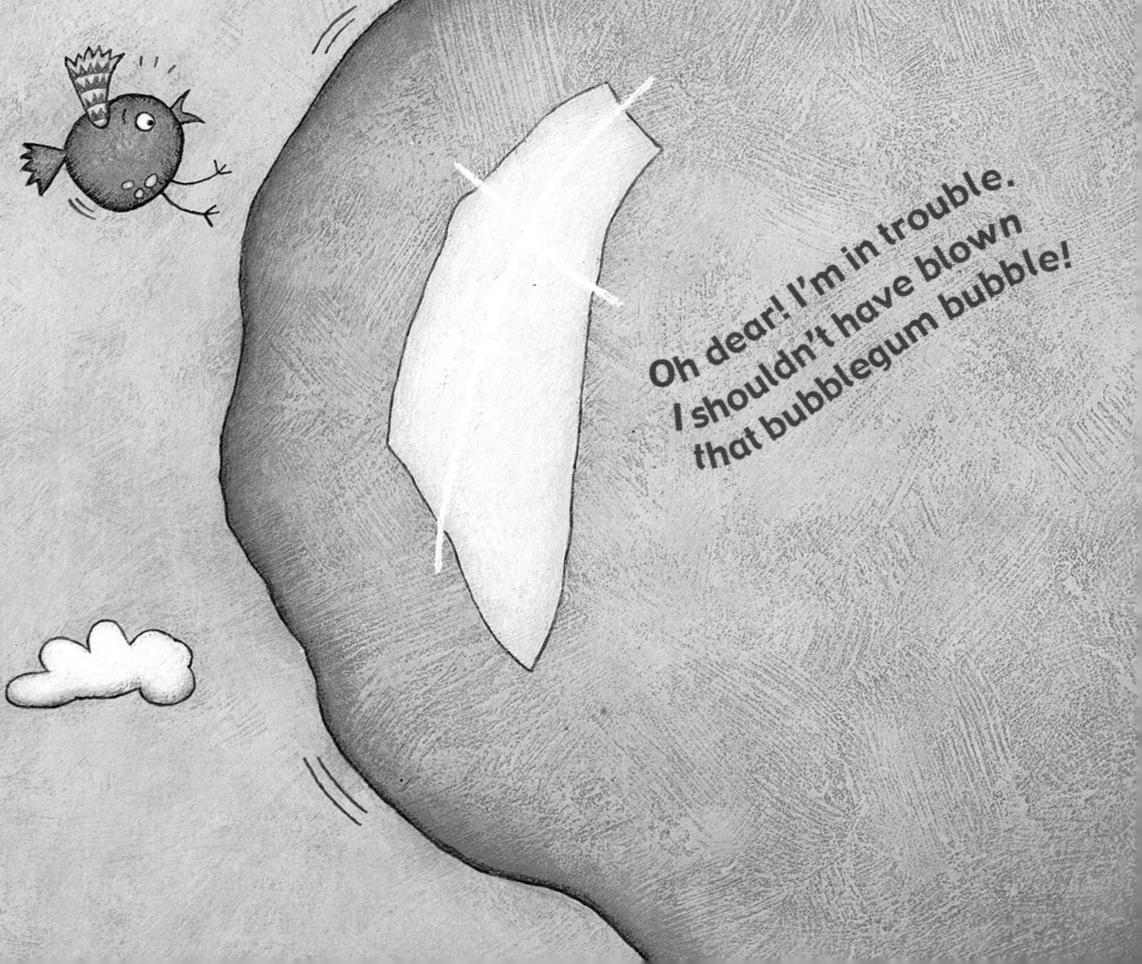

Oh dear! I'm in trouble.
I shouldn't have blown
that bubblegum bubble!

brother
rhyming sound -other

another   mother   other   smother

bubble
rhyming sound -ubble

rubble   stubble

-ubble also rhymes with *-ouble*
double   trouble

Cc

a
b
c
d
e
f
g
h
i
j
k
l
m
n
o
p
q
r
s
t
u
v
w
x
y
z

car   *rhyming sound -ar*

afar   ajar   bar   caviar   cigar   far   guitar   jaguar
jar   scar   spar   star   tar   tsar

Other words that rhyme with *car*
are   aha   baa   bizarre   ha   ha-ha   ma   pa

A jaguar from Zanzibar
Learned to play the bass guitar.
Now he's a famous movie star
And drives round in a racing car!

cart

rhyming sound -art

apart art chart dart depart heart part
smart start tart

catch

rhyming sound -atch

attach batch detach hatch latch match
mis-match patch scratch snatch thatch

cave
rhyming sound -ave

behave   brave   crave   forgave   gave   grave
heatwave   knave   microwave   pave   rave   save   shave
shockwave   slave   wave

"Behave!" said the queen to the knave.
"Or you'll drive me to an early grave!"

coat
rhyming sound -oat

afloat   boat   float   gloat   goat   moat   oat
stoat   throat

-oat rhymes with *-ote*
devote   dote   note   promote   quote
remote   vote   wrote

cook

rhyming sound -ook

book   brook   crook   hook   look   mistook   nook   rook
shook   took

My hands shook
When I saw the evil look
In the eyes of Captain Hook
As he **leapt** from the
page of my book.

At dawn I saw a unicorn.
I watched it grazing on the lawn,
The sunlight glinting on its horn.

corn   *rhyming sound -orn*

acorn   adorn   born   forlorn   horn   morn   scorn
shorn   sworn   thorn   torn   unicorn   worn

-orn rhymes with *-awn*
dawn   drawn   fawn   frogspawn
lawn   pawn   sawn   yawn

Other words that rhyme with *corn*
airbourne   bourne   leprechaun

cow

rhyming sound -ow

allow   bow   bow-wow   brow   eyebrow   how   meow   now
ow   pow   row   sow   vow   wow

-ow rhymes with some *-ough* words
bough   plough

crab

rhyming sound -ab

cab   dab   drab   fab   flab   grab   jab   kebab   lab
nab   scab   slab   stab

You mustn't try to grab
A very bad-tempered crab.
For if you do,
I'm telling you,
Its pincers will give you a jab.

crash

rhyming sound -ash

ash bash cash clash dash flash gash gnash hash lash mash rash sash slapdash slash smash splash thrash trash whiplash

Lightning flash

Thunder crash

Winds lash

Trees thrash

Raindrops splash

Storms smash!

crept
rhyming sound -ept

accept   adept   except   inept   intercept   kept   slept
swept   wept

Other words that rhyme with *crept*
leapt   stepped

I slept in, so I crept in,
But Miss saw me, so I was kept in.

Dd

dad
rhyming sound -ad

bad clad fad glad had lad mad
nomad pad sad

Another word that rhymes with *dad*
add

"You're not a bad lad," said Dad.
"But your music drives me mad!"

dance
rhyming sound -ance

advance chance entrance France glance lance
prance stance trance

dark

rhyming sound -ark

aardvark   ark   bark   embark   hark   landmark
lark   mark   park   remark   shark   spark

"My bite is worse than my bark," said the shark.
"With my teeth I leave my mark!"

dinner
rhyming sound -inner

beginner   inner   sinner   spinner
thinner   winner

dog
rhyming sound -og

agog   bog   clog   cog   flog   fog   frog   grog
hog   jog   log   slog

-og also rhymes with some *-ogue* words
catalogue   monologue

dream
rhyming sound -eam

beam   cream   daydream   gleam
ice cream   scream   seam   steam
stream   team

-eam also rhymes with *-eem*
redeem   seem   teem

Other words that rhyme with *dream*
extreme   scheme   supreme   theme

a
b
c
d
e
f
g
h
i
j
k
l
m
n
o
p
q
r
s
t
u
v
w
x
y
z

dress   *rhyming sound -ess*

address   bless   chess   confess   cress   depress   distress
excess   express   guess   happiness   helpless   impress
kindness   less   loneliness   mess   oppress   possess   press
princess   progress   stress   success   tress   unless

Another word that rhymes with *dress*
yes

Nicola Nicholas couldn't care less.
Nicola Nicholas tore her dress.
Nicola Nicholas tore her knickers.
Now Nicola Nicholas is knickerless.

duck   *rhyming sound -uck*

buck   chuck   cluck   luck   muck   pluck
struck   stuck   suck   truck   tuck   yuck

dust   *rhyming sound -ust*

adjust   bust   crust   disgust
gust   just   must   rust
thrust   trust

31

Ee

ear *rhyming sound -ear*

appear   clear   dear   disappear   fear
gear   hear   near   rear   shear   smear
spear   tear

-ear rhymes with *-eer*

beer   buccaneer   career   cheer   deer   engineer   jeer
leer   mountaineer   musketeer   peer   pioneer   sheer
sneer   steer   veer   volunteer

-ear rhymes with *-ere*

atmosphere   here   mere   persevere
revere   severe   sincere

Other words that rhyme with *ear*

cashier   cavalier   frontier   gondolier
pier   souvenir   weir

**We all gave a cheer
as the wizard made our teacher
disappear.**

east
rhyming sound -east

beast   feast   least   yeast

-east rhymes with *-eased*
ceased   creased   deceased   greased
increased   released

elf
rhyming sound -elf

bookshelf   herself   himself   itself
myself   self   shelf   yourself

end
rhyming sound -end

ascend   attend   bend   blend   defend   depend
descend   extend   friend   intend   lend   mend   offend
pretend   recommend   send   spend   suspend   tend   trend

**Here lies Charlotte Cul-de-Sac,
A most annoying friend,
She used to drive me round the bend
Until she came to a dead end.**

ever
rhyming sound -ever

clever   forever   however   never   sever   whatever
whenever   wherever   whichever   whoever

a b c d e f g h i j k l m n o p q r s t u v w x y z

Ff

face
rhyming sound -ace

ace brace commonplace disgrace embrace
fireplace grace lace misplace pace place
race replace shoelace space trace

-ace rhymes with *-ase*
base bookcase case chase database
staircase suitcase

There was a young girl called Grace
Whose nose spread all over her face
She had very few kisses
And the reason for this is
There wasn't a suitable place.

find

rhyming sound -ind

behind   bind   blind   grind   kind   mind   remind
rewind   rind   unkind   wind

-ind rhymes with *-ined*
dined   fined   lined   mined   pined   whined

Another word that rhymes with *find*
signed

When you stand in a queue, it's not kind to remind anyone you're behind that you're behind their behind.

fire

rhyming sound -ire

admire   bonfire   desire   dire   empire   hire   inquire   inspire
quagmire   spire   squire   tire   umpire   vampire   wire

Other words that rhyme with *fire*
choir   flyer   friar   fryer   higher
liar   pyre   tyre

Here lies a foolish young squire
Who was the most terrible liar.
He collapsed one day
And passed away
From the heat of his pants on fire!

first
rhyming sound -irst

thirst

Other words that rhyme with *first*
burst cursed nursed rehearsed worst

fish
rhyming sound -ish

dish perish punish rubbish selfish
squish swish vanish wish

**Three selfish shellfish each had a wish.
The wish each selfish shellfish wished
was a selfish shellfish wish.**

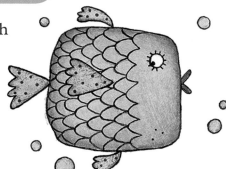

five
rhyming sound -ive

alive arrive dive drive hive jive live revive
strive survive

Another word that thymes with *five*
I've

flag
rhyming sound -ag

bag brag crag drag gag hag lag nag rag
sag snag stag swag tag wag zigzag

a
b
c
d
e
f
g
h
i
j
k
l
m
n
o
p
q
r
s
t
u
v
w
x
y
z

food *rhyming sound -ood*

brood   mood

-ood rhymes with *-ewed*
brewed   chewed   mewed   screwed   slewed   viewed

-ood also rhymes with *-ooed*
booed   boo-hooed   cooed   mooed   shampooed   shooed
tattooed   wooed

-ood also rhymes with *-ude*
altitude   attitude
crude   exclude
gratitude   include
intrude   nude
rude   solitude

-ood also rhymes
with *-ued*
argued
barbecued
glued   pursued
rescued   sued

fox

rhyming sound -ox

box   cox   ox   pox

-ox rhymes with *-ocks*

blocks   clocks   docks   flocks   frocks   knocks   locks   mocks
rocks   shocks   socks   stocks

Goldilocks wears pretty frocks
But I wish she'd change her   smelly socks.

a b c d e f g h i j k l m n o p q r s t u v w x y z

freeze

rhyming sound -eeze

breeze   sneeze   squeeze   wheeze

-eeze rhymes with *-ees*
agrees   bees   chimpanzees   degrees   dungarees   fees
flees   frees   knees   referees   sees   toffees   trees

-eeze also rhymes with *-ease*
disease   ease   please   tease

Other words that rhyme with *-eeze*
cheese   chimneys   donkeys   fleas   keys   monkeys
peas   seas   seize   skis   teas   these   trapeze

Chimpanzees in dungarees
Swing with ease on the trapeze,
While bees on skis
Struggle to juggle packs of peas.

a b c d e f g h i j k l m n o p q r s t u v w x y z

fur

rhyming sound -ur

blur   occur
slur   spur

-ur rhymes with *-ir*
fir   sir   stir

-ur also rhymes with *-er*
badger   her   otter
prefer   slipper   tiger

Always call a tiger "Sir"
And do not try to stroke his fur
For tigers are well known to grrr!

Other words that rhyme with *fur*
purr   were   whirr

a b c d e f g h i j k l m n o p q r s t u v w x y z

44

Gg

gate

rhyming sound -ate

appreciate   ate   calculate   celebrate   concentrate   confiscate
crate   create   date   debate   decorate   educate   estate
estimate   exaggerate   fascinate   fate   frustrate   grate   hate
investigate   irritate   Kate   late   mate   operate   plate   rate
separate   skate   slate   state

-ate rhymes with *-ait*
bait   wait

Other words that rhyme with *gate*
eight   fete   great   straight   weight

Elephant! Elephant!
Don't try to skate.
The ice is too thin,
It won't bear your
weight...

Too late!

45

girl
rhyming sound -irl

swirl   twirl   whirl

-irl rhymes with *-url*
curl   furl   hurl   unfurl

Other words that rhyme with *girl*
earl   pearl

glass
rhyming sound -ass

brass   bypass   class   grass   pass   trespass

grape
rhyming sound -ape

agape   ape   cape   drape   escape   gape
landscape   scrape   shape   tape

grub

rhyming sound -ub

club   cub   dub   hub   hubbub   pub   rub   scrub   shrub
snub   stub   tub

A grubby grub sat in a tub
And sang as he had a good scrub:

"I'm a scrub-a-grub, rub-a-dub grub!"

Hh

hairy
rhyming sound -airy

airy   dairy   fairy

-airy rhymes with *-ary*
canary   contrary   Mary   scary   vary   wary

hand
rhyming sound -and

and   band   brand   expand   gland   grand   land
sand   stand   strand   understand

-and rhymes with *-anned*
banned   canned   fanned   manned   planned
scanned   spanned   tanned

hat
rhyming sound -at

acrobat aristocrat at bat brat cat chat combat fat flat gnat habitat mat pat pit-a-pat rat rat-a-tat-tat sat spat splat that vat wombat

There was a young fellow called Matt
Who wanted to look like a cat
His feet were like paws
With retractable claws
And whiskers grew out of his hat.

hen
rhyming sound -en

amen Ben den fen glen Ken Len men pen ten then when wren yen

Another word that rhymes with *hen*
again

hit
rhyming sound -it

admit bandit biscuit bit circuit culprit exit fit flit grit habit it kit knit lit nit omit orbit outfit permit pit quit rabbit sit spit split summit twit visit wit

hole

rhyming sound -ole

casserole   console   dole   mole   pole   role
sole   stole   tadpole   vole   whole

-ole rhymes with *-oal*
coal   foal   goal   shoal

-ole also rhymes with some *-oll* words
poll   roll   scroll   stroll   troll

Other words that rhyme with *hole*
bowl   control   soul

Old King Cole scored a *very fine* **goal**
A very fine goal scored he.
A TV poll reckoned King Cole's goal
Was the best you'd ever see.

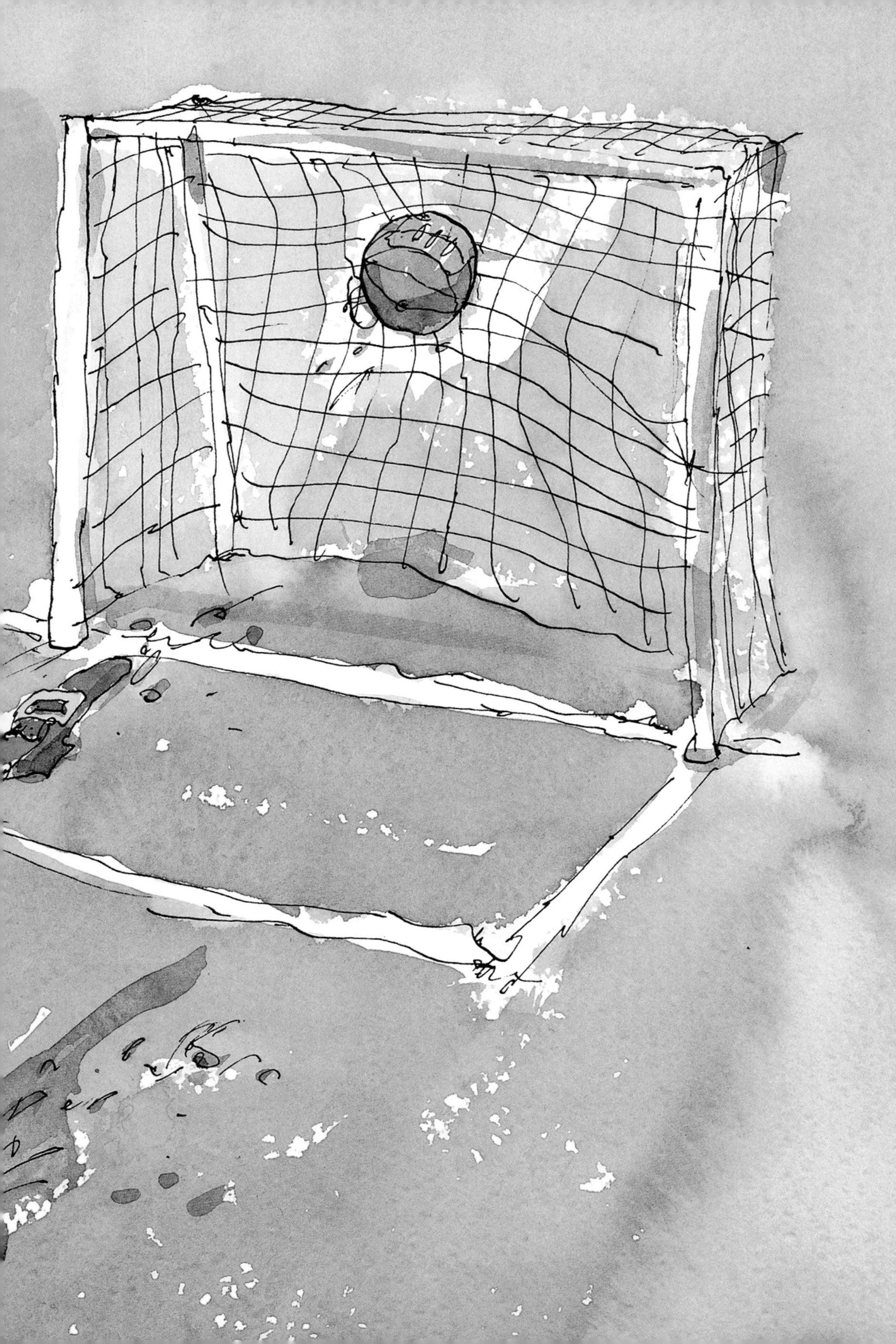

a
b
c
d
e
f
g
h
i
j
k
l
m
n
o
p
q
r
s
t
u
v
w
x
y
z

honey

rhyming sound -oney

money

-oney rhymes with *-unny*

bunny   funny   runny   sunny

I eat my peas with honey.
I've done it all my life.
It makes the peas taste funny.
But it keeps them on the knife.

hood   *rhyming sound -ood*

childhood   deadwood   driftwood   falsehood   good
neighbourhood   stood   understood   wood

-ood rhymes with some *-ould* words
could   should   would

hoop   *rhyming sound -oop*

coop   droop   loop   nincompoop
scoop   sloop   snoop   stoop
swoop   troop   whoop

-oop rhymes with *-oup*
group   soup

house   *rhyming sound -ouse*

louse   mouse   spouse

A mouse and his spouse doing cartwheels round the house.

hunt

rhyming sound -unt

blunt   grunt   punt   runt   shunt   stunt

Another word that rhymes with *hunt*
front

hut

rhyming sound -ut

but   chestnut   cut   doughnut   glut   gut
jut   nut   rut   shut   strut   tut-tut

Another word that rhymes
with *hut*
putt

Ii

ice
rhyming sound -ice

advice   dice   lice   mice   nice   price   rice   sacrifice   slice
spice   splice   trice   twice   vice

The three blind mice said,
"It's not very nice
Of the farmer's wife
To want to slice
Off our tails with her carving knife!"

Other words that
rhyme with *ice*
paradise
precise

ill

rhyming sound -ill

bill   brill   chill   drill   fill   frill   gill   grill   hill   Jill   kill
mill   pill   quill   shrill   sill   skill   spill   still   swill   thrill
till   will   windmill

-ill rhymes with *-il*
daffodil   fulfil   nil   Phil   tranquil   until

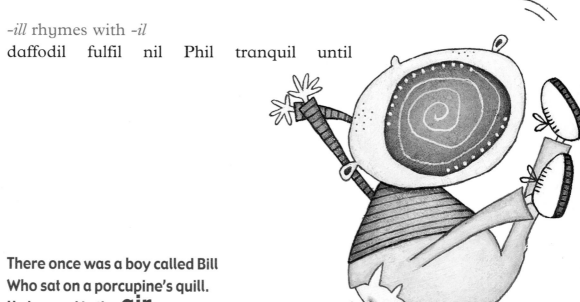

There once was a boy called Bill
Who sat on a porcupine's quill.
He jumped in the **air**
'Cause his bottom was bare
And that's why he cannot sit still.

imp
rhyming sound -imp

himp   crimp   limp   primp   scrimp
shrimp   skimp   wimp

ink
rhyming sound -ink

blink   brink   chink   clink   drink   kink   link   mink
pink   rink   shrink   sink   slink   stink   think   wink

itch
rhyming sound -itch

ditch   glitch   hitch   pitch   snitch
stitch   switch   twitch   witch

-itch rhymes with *-ich*
ostrich   rich   which

There were twin witches, Mitch and Titch.
No one could tell which witch was which.

a b c d e f g h i j k l m n o p q r s t u v w x y z

Jj

jam
rhyming sound -am

am   cram   dam   exam   gram   ham
Pam   pram   program   ram   Sam   scam
scram   sham   slam   swam   tram   wham
wigwam   yam

Another word that rhymes with *jam*
lamb

jet
rhyming sound -et

alphabet   basket   bet   bracelet   bucket   carpet   clarinet
cricket   duet   fidget   forget   fret   gadget   get   helmet
internet   jacket   let   magnet   met   net   pet   pocket
puppet   regret   rocket   secret   set   ticket   trumpet   upset
vet   wet   yet

-et rhymes with some *-eat* words
sweat   threat

-et also rhymes with *-ette*
baguette   cassette   courgette   launderette
omelette   serviette

Another word that rhymes with *jet*
debt

job
rhyming sound -ob

blob   bob   cob   gob   hob   hobnob   knob   lob   mob
rob   snob   sob   throb

jug
rhyming sound -ug

bug   chug   drug   dug   glug   hug   humbug   lug   mug
plug   rug   shrug   slug   smug   snug   thug   tug

A slimy slug drank from a jug.
A grubby bug drank from a mug.

Then the slug gave the *bug* a hug!

jump
rhyming sound -ump

bump   clump   dump   frump   goosebump   hump
lump   plump   pump   rump   slump   stump
thump   trump

a
b
c
d
e
f
g
h
i
j
k
l
m
n
o
p
q
r
s
t
u
v
w
x
y
z

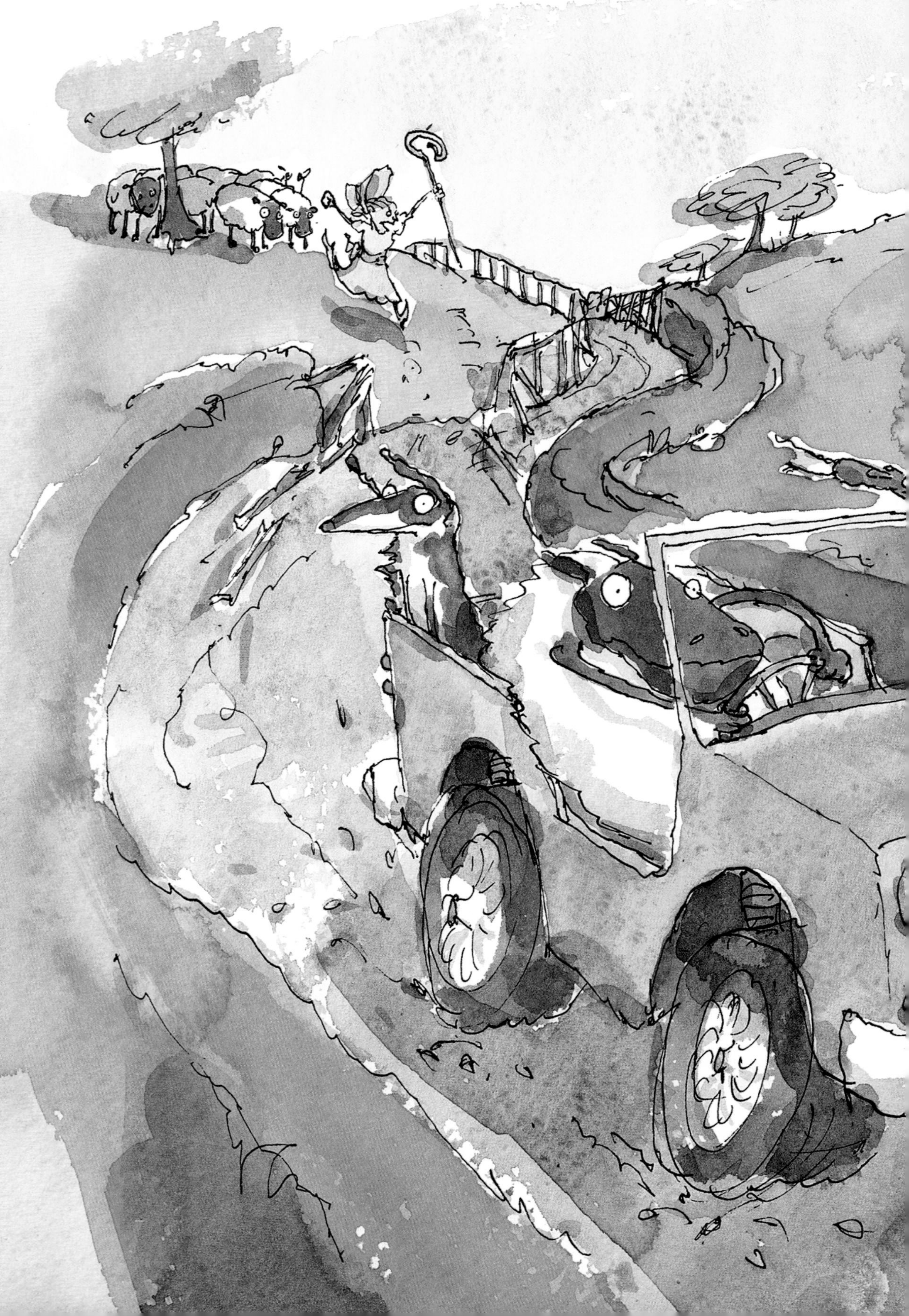

Kk

keep
rhyming sound -eep

asleep beep bleep cheep creep deep jeep
peep seep sheep sleep steep sweep weep

-eep rhymes with *-eap*
cheap heap leap reap

I'm a runaway sheep.
I stole the keys to Bo Peep's jeep
While she was lying fast asleep.
Get out of my way! **Beep! Beep!**

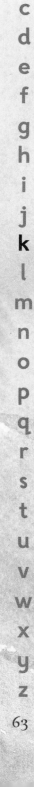

king

rhyming sound -ing

boring   bring   ceiling   cling   ding   fling   ping   ring
sing   sling   spring   sting   string   swing   thing   wing
wring   zing

When the bee gave the king a sting
The king did a highland fling.
So his arm ended up in a sling.

kiss

rhyming sound -iss

amiss   bliss   dismiss   hiss   kiss   miss

Other words that rhyme with *kiss*
liquorice   office   practice   promise   service   this

I'll be good, Mum, just promise me this:
You won't try to give me a kiss
In the playground. Just give it a miss!

knock

rhyming sound -ock

block   clock   crock   dock   flock   frock   lock   mock
rock   shock   sock   stock   tick-tock

a
b
c
d
e
f
g
h
i
j
k
l
m
n
o
p
q
r
s
t
u
v
w
x
y
z

Ll

lake
rhyming sound -ake

awake   bake   brake   cake   drake   fake   flake   make
mistake   pancake   quake   rake   sake   shake   snake
snowflake   stake   take   wake

-ake rhymes with some *-eak* words
break   steak

Other words that rhyme with *lake*
ache   headache
toothache

last
rhyming sound -ast

aghast   blast   cast   contrast   fast   mast
past   vast

-ast rhymes with *-assed*
classed   passed

"You'd better run fast," said the pirate to Frank.
"The last past the mast will walk the plank!"

leg
rhyming sound -eg

beg   dreg   Greg   keg   Meg   nutmeg   peg

Another word that rhymes with *leg*
egg

lid
rhyming sound -id

bid   did   forbid   grid   hid   liquid   kid   pyramid   quid
rapid   rid   rigid   skid   slid   squid   stupid   timid   undid

I slid back the bolt and undid the locks
To see what lay hidden in the secret box.

light
rhyming sound -ight

bright　delight　fight　flight　fright　knight　midnight
might　night　outright　playwright　plight　right　sight
slight　stagefright　tight　tonight　twilight　upright　uptight

-ight rhymes with *-ite*

appetite　bite　dynamite　excite　ignite　invite　kite　mite
polite　quite　recite　site　spite　sprite　unite　website
white　write

Other words that rhyme with *light*
byte　height

When Dwight Wright had stagefright,
Mrs Wright said, "Don't get uptight, Dwight,
It'll be all right on the night."

After the first night, Dwight Wright
Said, "It went all right.
You were quite right, Mrs Wright."

lord

afford   chord   cord   ford   record   sword

-ord rhymes with *-oard*
aboard   board   cardboard   hoard   keyboard
scoreboard   skateboard

-ord also rhymes with *-ored*
adored   bored   explored   ignored   scored   snored   stored

Other words that rhyme with *lord*
abroad   applaud   award   broad   horde   poured   reward
roared   soared   toward   ward

The crowd roared and began to applaud
As the young lord drew his sword,
Slew the monster and claimed the reward.

a
b
c
d
e
f
g
h
i
j
k
l
m
n
o
p
q
r
s
t
u
v
w
x
y
z

love
rhyming sound -ove

above   dove   glove   shove

lunch
rhyming sound -unch

brunch   bunch   crunch   hunch   munch   punch   scrunch

lung
rhyming sound -ung

bung   clung   dung   flung   hung   rung   slung   sprung
strung   stung   sung   swung   wrung

Other words that rhyme with *lung*
among   tongue   young

70

Mm

map *rhyming sound -ap*

bap   cap   chap   clap   flap   gap   kidnap   lap   nap
overlap   rap   sap   scrap   slap   snap   strap   tap
trap   unwrap   wrap   yap   zap

On the Clip Clop Clap
All the Flops flip flap
And the Bongles boogle in the breeze.
The Sniggers snip snap
The Trotters trip trap
And the Somersaults sniff and sneeze
The Somersaults sniff and sneeze.

meat

rhyming sound -eat

beat   bleat   cheat   defeat   eat   feat   heat   neat
peat   pleat   repeat   retreat   seat   treat   wheat

-eat rhymes with *-eet*
discreet   feet   fleet   greet   meet   parakeet   sheet
sleet   street   sweet

-eat also rhymes with some *-ete* words
athlete   compete   complete   concrete   delete

Pete dressed up in a sheet
And went round the street
Knocking on doors
Saying, **"Trick or treat?"**

But at number thirty four
Pete got more
Than he bargained for,
When a troll opened the door!

So Pete beat a hasty retreat.

merry
rhyming sound -erry

berry   cherry   ferry   Terry

Other words that rhyme with *merry*
bury   very

middle
rhyming sound -iddle

diddle   fiddle   griddle   riddle   twiddle

Hey diddle riddle
The first is in first
The rest is in middle!

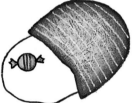

a
b
c
d
e
f
g
h
i
j
k
l
m
n
o
p
q
r
s
t
u
v
w
x
y
z

mist *rhyming sound -ist*

cyclist   fist   insist   list   resist   tourist   twist   wrist

-ist rhymes with *-issed*
dismissed   hissed   kissed   missed

mix *rhyming sound -ix*

fix   matrix   phoenix   six

-ix rhymes with *-icks*
bricks   broomsticks   chicks   clicks   flicks   gimmicks
kicks   licks   matchsticks   nicks   picks   pricks   sticks
ticks   tricks

The ghost of the conjuror said,
"I'm really in a fix.
The problem is the audience
Sees right through all my tricks."

moon *rhyming sound -oon*

afternoon   baboon   balloon   bassoon
cartoon   croon   harpoon   honeymoon
lagoon   macaroon   maroon   noon
platoon   raccoon   saloon   soon
spoon   swoon   tycoon   typhoon

A baboon in a saloon playing a tune on a bassoon.

-oon rhymes with *-une*

dune   fortune   June   Neptune   prune   tune

Another word that rhymes with *moon*

strewn

mum
mud — *rhyming sound -ud*

bud   cud   dud   scud   spud
stud   sud   thud

Other words that rhyme
with *mud*
blood   flood

mum — *rhyming sound -um*

chum   drum   glum   gum   hum
plum   rum   scrum   scum   slum
strum   sum   swum   tum   yum
yum-yum

-um rhymes with *-umb*

crumb   dumb   numb   plumb
succumb   thumb

Other words that rhyme with *mum*
become   come   some

a
b
c
d
e
f
g
h
i
j
k
l
m
n
o
p
q
r
s
t
u
v
w
x
y
z

Nn

a b c d e f g h i j k l m n o p q r s t u v w x y z

name

rhyming sound -ame

became   blame   came   fame   flame   frame   game
lame   same   shame   tame

-ame rhymes with *-aim*
acclaim   aim   claim   exclaim   maim

I am the wizard's dragon.
I speak with tongues of flame.
I am the wizard's dragon.
Firesnorter is my name.

a
b
c
d
e
f
g
h
i
j
k
l
m
n
o
p
q
r
s
t
u
v
w
x
y
z

neck
rhyming sound -eck

beck   check   deck   fleck   peck   speck   wreck

Other words that rhyme with *neck*
cheque   Czech   discotheque   high-tech   trek

"Just let me check," said the vampire.
"I think there's a speck
Of blood on your neck."

nettle
rhyming sound -ettle

fettle   kettle   settle

-ettle rhymes with *-etal*
metal   petal

78

nine

rhyming sound -ine

airline   brine   combine   define   dine   divine   fine   line
mine   pine   recline   shine   shrine   spine   swine   twine
valentine   vine   whine   wine

-ine rhymes with *-ign*
design   resign   sign

It sent a shiver down my spine
When I received a valentine,
Saying, "I think you are divine"
'Cause it was signed 'Frankenstein'!

nose   *rhyming sound -ose*

chose   close   expose   hose   pose   propose   prose   rose
suppose   those

-ose rhymes with *-ows*
arrows   bellows   blows   bows   bungalows   crows   elbows
flows   glows   grows   knows   meadows   mows   rows
shadows   shows   slows   snows   sows   stows   throws   tows

-ose also rhymes with *-oes*
foes   goes   hoes   toes   woes   oboes
volcanoes   tiptoes   dominoes   potatoes

-ose also rhymes with some *-os* words
radios   stereos   videos

Other words that rhyme with *nose*
bulldoze   doze   froze
sews   UFOs

When the winter wind blows
An icicle grows on the scarecrow's nose
And it looks just like Pinnochio's!

Oo

oak   *rhyming sound -oak*

cloak   croak   soak

-oak rhymes with *-oke*
awoke   bloke   broke   choke   coke
joke   poke   provoke   smoke   spoke
stroke   woke   yoke

Other words that rhyme with *oak*
folk   yolk

oil   *rhyming sound -oil*

boil   broil   coil   foil   recoil   soil   spoil
toil   turmoil

-oil rhymes with *-oyal*
loyal   royal

Another word that rhymes
with *oil*
gargoyle

old

rhyming sound -old

behold   bold   cold   fold   gold   hold   marigold   scaffold
scold   sold   told

Other words that rhyme with *old*
bowled   cajoled   consoled   controlled   mould   patrolled
polled   rolled   soled   strolled

"Behold!" said the wizard
And he conjured a room full of gold.
But my blood ran cold,
When he warned,
"My secrets must never be told."

out

about   blackout   bout   clout   dugout   hideout
knockout   lookout   lout   pout   rout   scout
shootout   shout   snout   spout   sprout   stout
throughout   trout   without

Other words that rhyme with *out*
doubt   drought

owl

fowl   growl   howl   prowl   scowl   yowl

-owl rhymes with *-owel*
bowel   towel   trowel   vowel

Another word that rhymes
with *owl*
foul

Pp

page   *rhyming sound -age*

age   cage   engage   enrage   outrage   rage
rampage   sage   stage   teenage   upstage   wage

"It's like being on stage.
Let me out or pay me a wage!"
The monkey screeched in a rage
As it rattled the bars of its cage.

paint
rhyming sound -aint

complaint   faint   quaint   saint   taint

paste
rhyming sound -aste

haste   taste   waste

-aste rhymes with *-aced*
braced   disgraced   embraced   faced   graced   laced   paced
placed   raced   replaced   spaced   traced

Other words that rhyme with *paste*
chased   waist

pond
rhyming sound -ond

beyond   blond   bond   fond   respond

Another word that rhymes with *pond*
wand

Said the frog in the pond,
"Please kiss me or wave your wand."
But the princess didn't respond.

a
b
c
d
e
f
g
h
i
j
k
l
m
n
o
p
q
r
s
t
u
v
w
x
y
z

pool

cool   drool   fool   school   spool   stool
toadstool   tool   whirlpool

-ool rhymes with *-ule*
capsule   globule   miniscule   molecule
mule   ridicule   rule   schedule   yule

Other words that rhyme with *pool*
fuel   ghoul

In our school
There's an empty stool
Where nobody sits
Except the ghoul
Of the pupil who died
While playing the fool.

post

almost   ghost   host   most
signpost   utmost

-ost rhymes with *-oast*
boast   coast
roast   toast

At the Halloween Ball
Our host was a ghost
Who walked through the wall.

a b c d e f g h i j k l m n o p q r s t u v w x y z

86

pot

rhyming sound -ot

apricot   blot   cannot   clot   cot   dot   earshot   forgot   got
hot   jackpot   jot   knot   lot   mascot   not   plot   robot   rot
Scot   shot   slot   snot   spot   swot   tot   trot

Other words that rhyme with *pot*
squat   swat   what   yacht

Ned Nott was shot
And Sam Shott was not.
So it's better to be Shott than Nott.

print

rhyming sound -int

flint   footprint   glint
hint   lint   mint
skint   splint   sprint
squint   tint

a
b
c
d
e
f
g
h
i
j
k
l
m
n
o
p
q
r
s
t
u
v
w
x
y
z

puff *rhyming sound -uff*

bluff   buff   cuff   dandruff   duff   fluff   gruff   handcuff
huff   scruff   scuff   snuff   stuff

-uff rhymes with some *-ough* words
enough   rough   tough

pull *rhyming sound -ull*

bull   full

-ull rhymes with *-ul*
armful   awful   beautiful   careful   cheerful   doubtful
dreadful   faithful   fearful   graceful   harmful   hopeful
joyful   playful   useful   wonderful

Another word that rhymes with *pull*
wool

Qq

queen   *rhyming sound -een*

been   between   canteen   green   keen   preen   screen   seen
sheen   spleen   teen   thirteen   fourteen (etc)

-een rhymes with *-ean*
bean   clean   glean   Jean   lean   mean   wean

-een also rhymes with some *-ine* words
limousine   magazine   routine   sardine   tangerine   trampoline

-een also rhymes with *-ene*
gene   hygiene   scene   serene

"I'm a queen," said Kathleen.
"We've been filming a scene.
That's my picture in a magazine
And over there's my limousine."
"Dream on," said Jean.

quick   *rhyming sound -ick*

brick   chick   click   flick   gimmick   kick   lick   limerick
pick   prick   sick   slick   stick   thick   tick   trick   wick

-ick rhymes with *-ic*
attic   basic   comic   elastic   electric   fantastic   frantic
garlic   lunatic   magic   music   panic   picnic   plastic   public
supersonic   terrific   tragic

Rr

rain
rhyming sound -ain

again   brain   chain   complain   contain   drain   entertain
explain   gain   grain   main   obtain   pain   plain   refrain
remain   Spain   sprain   stain   strain   train   vain

-ain rhymes with *-ane*
cane   crane   Jane   lane   mane   pane   plane   sane   vane

Other words that rhyme with *rain*
rein   vein   reign

There was a young girl called Elaine
Who was dreadfully sick on the train –
Not once but again and again!

red

bed bled bred fed fled led moped quadruped red
shed shred sled sped Ted wed

-ed rhymes with some *-ead* words
ahead bread dead dread head instead lead read
spread thread tread widespread

Another word that rhymes with *red*
said

"I sped down the hill on my sled,"
But I crashed and demolished the shed,"
Said Ted, as he lay on the bed
Feeling the bump on his head.

ride

rhyming sound -ide

aside   astride   beside   bride   collide   countryside   decide
divide   glide   guide   hide   inside   pride   provide   side
slide   stride   tide   wide

-ide rhymes with some *-ied* words
cried   defied   denied   died   dried   fried   horrified   lied
spied   terrified   tied   tried

Other words that rhyme with *ride*
dyed   eyed   I'd   sighed

river

rhyming sound -iver

deliver   liver   quiver   shiver   sliver

It made me shake.
It made me shiver.
When the highwayman's ghost
Shouted,
"Stand and deliver!"

a
b
c
d
e
f
g
h
i
j
k
l
m
n
o
p
q
r
s
t
u
v
w
x
y
z

93

road *rhyming sound -oad*

goad   load   toad

-oad rhymes with *-ode*
code   episode   erode   explode   mode   ode   rode   strode

-oad also rhymes with some *-owed* words
burrowed   crowed   flowed   glowed   mowed   owed   rowed
showed   slowed   snowed   stowed   towed

Here lies the body of a toad,
Who forgot his Highway Code.
He didn't wait till the traffic slowed,
Before he tried to cross the road.

room

rhyming sound -oom

bloom   boom   bridegroom   broom   doom   gloom   groom
heirloom   loom   mushroom   zoom

-oom rhymes with *-ume*
costume   flume   fume   perfume   plume

Other words that rhyme with *room*
tomb   whom   womb

A skeleton once in Khartoum
Invited a ghost to his room
They spent the whole night
In the eeriest fight
As to who should be frightened of whom.

rope   *rhyming sound -ope*

antelope   cope   dope   elope   envelope   grope   hope
horoscope   lope   microscope   mope   pope   scope   slope
telescope   tightrope

Another word that rhymes with *rope*
soap

**"I hope I can cope," said the antelope
as it started to walk along the tightrope.**

round   *rhyming sound -ound*

around   astound   background   bound
found   ground   hound   mound   pound
profound   sound   surround   wound

-ound rhymes with *-owned*
browned   clowned   crowned   downed   drowned
frowned   renowned

**My heart begins to pound
As I spin round and round,
On the whirling, twirling wheel
And I wish I was on the ground!**

rumble   *rhyming sound -umble*

bumble   crumble   fumble   grumble
humble   jumble   mumble   stumble   tumble

rush
rhyming sound -ush

blush   brush   crush   flush   gush   hush   lush   mush
plush   shush   slush   thrush

a
b
c
d
e
f
g
h
i
j
k
l
m
n
o
p
q
r
s
t
u
v
w
x
y
z

Ss

score   *rhyming sound -ore*

adore   ashore   before   bore   carnivore   chore   core   encore
explore   galore   gore   ignore   more   ore   pore   shore
snore   sore   store   swore   therefore   tore   wore

-ore rhymes with *-oar*
boar   oar   roar   soar

-ore also rhymes with *-aw*
caw   claw   draw   flaw   gnaw   guffaw   jackdaw
jaw   law   outlaw   paw   raw   saw   seesaw   straw   thaw

Other words that rhyme with *score*
corridor   dinosaur   door
drawer   floor   for   four
indoor   meteor   nor
or   outdoor   pour
war   your

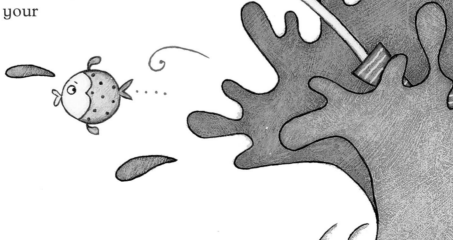

shirt
rhyming sound -irt

dirt   flirt   skirt   squirt

-irt rhymes with *-urt*
blurt   curt   hurt   spurt

-irt also rhymes with *-ert*
advert   alert   Bert   concert   desert
dessert   expert   pert

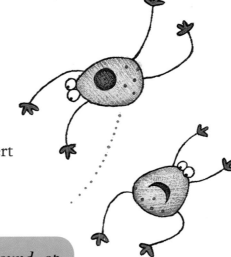

shop
rhyming sound -op

bop   chop   clop   cop   crop   drop   flip-flop   flop
hop   lollipop   lop   mop   plop   pop   prop   shop
slop   stop   top

Another word that rhymes
with *shop*
swap

When the giant dived in the lake
There was an enormous plop,
And water flew up everywhere
'Cause he did a belly-flop.

a
b
c
d
e
f
g
h
i
j
k
l
m
n
o
p
q
r
s
t
u
v
w
x
y
z

smile   *rhyming sound -ile*

agile   awhile   crocodile   file   fragile
hostile   mile   missile   mobile   pile   profile
reptile   stile   tile   vile   while

Other words that rhyme with *smile*
aisle   dial   I'll   isle   style   trial

"I'll dine in style," said the crocodile,
Giving a smile,
As he sharpened his teeth with a file.

snow   *rhyming sound -ow*

arrow   below   blow   bow   burrow   crow   elbow   flow
glow   grow   hedgerow   know   low   marrow   meadow   mow
pillow   rainbow   row   scarecrow   shadow   shallow   show
slow   sorrow   sow   stow   throw   tomorrow   tow   window

-ow rhymes with *-o*
ago   armadillo   buffalo   commando   disco   domino   echo
go   halo   hello   hero   hippo   logo   macho   mosquito   no
patio   photo   piano   potato   radio   rodeo   so   solo   stereo
studio   tornado   UFO   video   volcano   yo-yo   zero

-ow also rhymes with *-oe*
doe   foe   hoe   Joe   mistletoe   oboe   toe   woe

Other words that rhyme with *snow*
although   dough   owe   sew   though

song
rhyming sound -ong

along belong bong ding-dong
dong gong long oblong pong
prong sarong strong throng
tong wrong

spade
rhyming sound -ade

arcade barricade blade decade evade fade
grade invade jade lemonade made
marmalade parade persuade shade
trade wade

-ade rhymes with *-aid*

afraid aid braid laid maid mermaid paid
raid staid

-ade also rhymes with *-ayed*

arrayed betrayed decayed delayed frayed played
prayed sprayed stayed strayed swayed X-rayed

Other words that rhyme with *spade*
neighed obeyed preyed suede surveyed weighed

Jade shook the bottle of lemonade,
Then she opened it and we all got sprayed.

speak
rhyming sound -eak

beak   bleak   creak   freak   leak   peak   sneak
squeak   streak   weak

-eak rhymes with *-eek*
cheek   creek   Greek   leek   meek   peek   reek   seek
sleek   week

-eak also rhymes with *-ique*
antique   boutique   clique   technique   unique

Another word that rhymes with *speak*
shriek

Two ghosts are playing hide-and-shriek.
They've been seeking each other since last week.

102

sport

airport   export   fort   import   passport   port   report
resort   short   snort   sort   support   transport

> Sean Short bought some shorts,
> The shorts were shorter than
> Sean Short thought.
> Sean Short's short shorts were so short
> Sean Short thought, "Sean you ought
> Not to have bought shorts so short."

-ort rhymes with *-aught*
caught   distraught   fraught   onslaught   taught

-ort also rhymes with *-ought*
bought   brought   fought   nought   ought
sought   thought

-ort rhymes with some *-art* words
quart   thwart   wart

Other words that rhyme with *sport*
astronaut   court   juggernaut   taut

a
b
c
d
e
f
g
h
i
j
k
l
m
n
o
p
q
r
s
t
u
v
w
x
y
z

103

stamp
rhyming sound -amp

amp   camp   champ   clamp   cramp
damp   lamp   ramp   scamp   tramp

storm
rhyming sound -orm

dorm   form   norm   perform   uniform

-orm rhymes with some *-arm* words
swarm   warm

sun

sun *rhyming sound -un*

begun   bun   fun   gun   nun   pun   run   shun   spun   stun

-un rhymes with some *-one* words
done   none   one   someone

-un also rhymes with some *-on* words
son   ton   won

A rabbit raced a turtle.
The turtle easily won.
The rabbit came in second,
A little hot cross bun.

swim

swim *rhyming sound -im*

brim   dim   grim   him   Jim   Kim   prim   rim   skim   slim
Tim   trim   whim

Other words that rhyme with *swim*
gym   hymn   limb   pseudonym   synonym

105

Tt

table   *rhyming sound -able*

able   cable   fable   stable   timetable

Another word that rhymes with *table*
label

tail   *rhyming sound -ail*

ail   bail   detail   fail   frail   hail   jail   mail   nail   pail
quail   rail   sail   snail   trail   wail

-ail rhymes with *-ale*
ale   bale   dale   exhale   female   gale   impale   inhale
male   nightingale   pale   sale   scale   stale   tale
telltale   whale

Another word that rhymes with *tail*
veil

A whale in a veil getting married in a gale.

talk   *rhyming sound -alk*

chalk   stalk   walk

-alk rhymes with *-ork*
cork   fork   pork   stork

-alk also rhymes with *-awk*
gawk   hawk   squawk   tomahawk

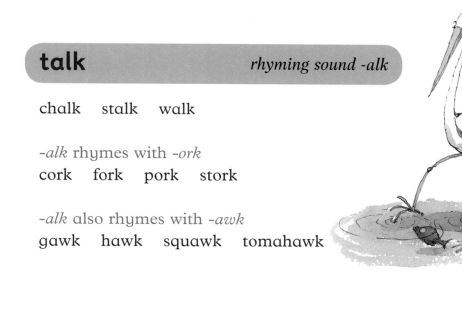

a
b
c
d
e
f
g
h
i
j
k
l
m
n
o
p
q
r
s
t
u
v
w
x
y
z

tent

rhyming sound -ent

accident ascent bent cement cent compliment
consent content dent descent dissent event experiment
fragment frequent invent lent ornament present prevent
recent relent rent resent scent sent spent torment
vent went

-ent rhymes with some *-eant* words
leant meant

We could not get rid of the scent
That a cow had left outside the tent!

a
b
c
d
e
f
g
h
i
j
k
l
m
n
o
p
q
r
s
t
u
v
w
x
y
z

tickle
rhyming sound -ickle

fickle   pickle   prickle   sickle   trickle

Another word that rhymes with *tickle*
icicle

Don't tickle a thistle or you'll get in a pickle,
For thistles are prickly and thistles'll prickle.

a
b
c
d
e
f
g
h
i
j
k
l
m
n
o
p
q
r
s
t
u
v
w
x
y
z

tie

rhyming sound -ie

die   lie   pie   untie

-ie rhymes with some *-y words*

ally   butterfly   by   cry   deny   dry   fly   fry   horrify
July   lay-by   lullaby   magnify   multiply   my   mystify
nearby   petrify   pigsty   pry   rely   reply   satisfy   shy
sky   sly   spy   sty   supply   terrify   try   why   wry

-ie also rhymes with *-igh*

high   sigh   thigh

Other words that rhyme with *tie*

alibi   buy   bye   dye   eye   goodbye   guy   I

Georgie Porgie shouted "Hi!"
To a girl as she passed by.
"Give me a kiss. Don't be shy."
"Give you a kiss! I'd rather die."

time
rhyming sound -ime

chime   crime   grime   lime   mime   pantomime
prime   slime

Other words that rhyme with *time*
climb   enzyme   I'm   rhyme   thyme

tower
rhyming sound -ower

cauliflower   cower   flower   glower   power   shower

-ower rhymes with some *-our* words
devour   flour   hour   our   scour   sour

a
b
c
d
e
f
g
h
i
j
k
l
m
n
o
p
q
r
s
t
u
v
w
x
y
z

town
rhyming sound -own

brown   clown   crown   down   drown   frown   gown

Another word that rhymes with *town*
noun

toy
rhyming sound -oy

ahoy   alloy   annoy   boy   buoy   convoy   corduroy
cowboy   coy   destroy   employ   enjoy   joy   ploy   Roy

tree
rhyming sound -ee

agree   bee   chimpanzee   coffee   degree   disagree   fee
flee   free   glee   guarantee   jamboree   jubilee   knee
marquee   pedigree   referee   refugee   see   settee   spree
tee   three   toffee   wee

-ee rhymes with *-ea*
flea   pea   plea   sea   tea

Other words that rhyme with *tree*
be   chimney   donkey   genie   grafitti
he   honey   key   macaroni   me   money
monkey   pixie   quay   recipe   she   ski
valley   we

trunk
rhyming sound -unk

bunk   chipmunk   chunk   clunk   drunk   dunk   hunk   junk
punk   shrunk   skunk   slunk   stunk   sunk

Another word that rhymes with *trunk*
monk

"After the skunk slunk over my bunk,
it stunk!" said the monk.

Uu

under
rhyming sound -under

blunder   plunder   thunder

Another word that rhymes with *under*
wonder

The pirates made a dreadful blunder
By trying to hide all their plunder
Beneath a tree during the thunder.
Now they're lying six feet under!

up
rhyming sound -up

buttercup   cup   hiccup   pickup   pup   sup

loot

114

urn

rhyming sound -urn

burn   churn   return   spurn   turn

-*urn* rhymes with -*earn*
earn   learn   yearn

-*urn* also rhymes with -*ern*
concern   fern   stern

us

rhyming sound -us

bonus   bus   cactus   circus   crocus   genius   hippopotamus
minus   octopus   plus   pus   radius   thus   virus   walrus

-*us* rhymes with some -*uss* words
discuss   fuss

-*us* also rhymes with -*ous*
anxious   callous   courageous   curious   dubious   enormous
envious   fabulous   famous   furious   glorious   gorgeous
hideous   hilarious   horrendous   ingenious   jealous   ludicrous
marvellous   mischievous   monstrous   mysterious   nervous
obvious   precious   raucous   ravenous   serious
tremendous   various   wondrous

**The driver caused an awful fuss
When we tried to board the bus
With our hippopotamus.**

use

rhyming sound -use

abuse   accuse   amuse   confuse   enthuse   excuse   fuse   muse   refuse   ruse

-use rhymes with *-ews*
chews   news   screws   stews

-use also rhymes with *-ues*
blues   clues   hues   queues

-use also rhymes with *-ooze*
booze   ooze   snooze

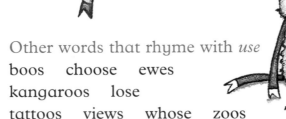

Other words that rhyme with *use*
boos   choose   ewes
kangaroos   lose
tattoos   views   whose   zoos

Gnus who choose to read the news
Share their views in queues in zoos.

Vv

van *rhyming sound -an*

an ban began bran can caravan catamaran clan
deadpan fan flan gran Japan man marzipan nan
orang-utan pan plan ran scan span Stan tan than

A young man who came from Japan
Taught his orang-utan to cancan.
When I asked if he can,
The young man from Japan
Said, "Can he cancan? Yes, he can!"

vest

rhyming sound -est

arrest   bequest   best   chest   conquest   contest
crest   detest   digest   guest   infest   invest   jest
lest   nest   pest   protest   quest   request   rest
suggest   test   west   zest

-est rhymes with *-essed*

addressed   blessed   caressed
confessed   depressed   digressed
distressed   dressed   expressed
guessed   impressed
messed   obsessed
possessed
pressed
progressed
stressed

Ww

wall   *rhyming sound -all*

all   ball   call   fall   football   hall   mall   pall   small
squall   stall   tall

-all rhymes with *-awl*
bawl   brawl   crawl
drawl   scrawl   shawl
sprawl   trawl

-all also rhymes with *-aul*
caterwaul   haul
maul   Paul

There was a young fellow called Paul
Who went to a fancy dress ball.
But he made a mistake
'Cause he went as a cake
And a dog ate him up in the hall.

119

weed
rhyming sound -eed

agreed bleed breed creed deed exceed freed
greed guaranteed heed indeed need proceed
reed refereed seed speed steed succeed tweed

-eed rhymes with some *-ead* words
bead knead lead plead read

-eed also rhymes with some *-ede* words
centipede concede millipede stampede swede

well
rhyming sound -ell

bell cell dwell farewell fell hell quell sell
shell smell spell swell tell unwell yell

Other words that rhyme with *well*
caramel carousel excel gel hotel
lapel motel parallel
propel rebel

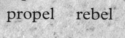

Spinning round on the carousel
Sound the horn and ring the bell.
Feel the fairground's magic spell
Spinning round on the carousel.

121

a
b
c
d
e
f
g
h
i
j
k
l
m
n
o
p
q
r
s
t
u
v
w
x
y
z

wheel   *rhyming sound -eel*

eel   feel   heel   keel   kneel   peel   reel   steel

-eel rhymes with *-eal*
appeal   conceal   deal   heal   ideal   meal   ordeal   peal
real   reveal   seal   squeal   steal   veal   zeal

win   *rhyming sound -in*

begin   bin   cabin   chin   coffin   din   dolphin   fin   goblin
gremlin   grin   in   javelin   kin   margin   muffin   origin
penguin   pin   puffin   pumpkin   robin   ruin   satin   sequin
shin   sin   skin   spin   thin   tin   twin
violin   vitamin   within

Other words that rhyme with *win*
examine   inn

**When Violet plays her violin
She makes a really awful din.
I'm glad she hasn't got a twin!**

wise

rhyming sound -ise

advertise   advise   apologise   arise   clockwise   disguise
exercise   guise   likewise   organise   prise   revise   rise
sunrise   surprise

-ise rhymes with some *-ies* words
cries   dies   dries   flies   fries   horrifies   lies   lullabies
petrifies   pies   replies   skies   spies   terrifies   ties   tries

-ise also rhymes with *-ize*
capsize   hypnotize   idolize   prize
realize   recognize   size

Other words that rhyme with *wise*
buys   eyes   highs   sighs   thighs

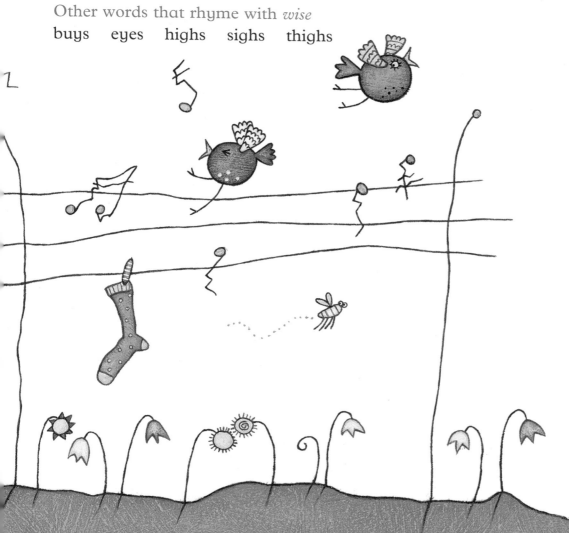

Xx

X-ray
rhyming sound -ay

alleyway anyway away bay betray birthday bray
clay day decay delay display essay fray hay
holiday hooray hurray lay may
midday Monday (etc) motorway OK
pay pray railway ray say spray
stay stowaway straightaway subway
sway takeaway today tray
way yesterday

-ay rhymes with *-eigh*
neigh sleigh weigh

-ay also rhymes with *-ey*
disobey grey hey obey
prey survey they

Other words that rhyme with *X-ray*
ballet bouquet buffet
cafe chalet croquet
duvet fiancé(e) paté
ricochet sachet

When Auntie Fay began to neigh
And spend the day just eating hay,
My uncle said, "I cannot say
Why she's behaving in this way.
I'd better put her in the stable
In the stall next to your Auntie Mabel."

Yy

yard — *rhyming sound -ard*

bard   bombard   card   discard   hard
lard   leotard   postcard   regard   shard

-ard rhymes with *-arred*
barred   charred   jarred   marred
scarred   sparred   starred   tarred

Another word that rhymes with *yard*
guard

yellow

rhyming sound -ellow

bellow   fellow   mellow

Other words that rhyme with *yellow*
cello   hello

I was practising playing the cello,
When I heard someone give a loud bellow,
"For goodness sake
You make my ears ache.
Please stop it. There's a good fellow!"

Zz

zip
rhyming sound -ip

blip championship chip clip dip drip equip fingertip
flip friendship gossip grip hardship hip kip leadership
lip microchip nip paperclip pip quip rip ship sip
skip slip snip strip tip trip tulip whip

zoo
rhyming sound -oo

a-choo bamboo boo coo cuckoo hullaballoo igloo
kangaroo loo moo shampoo shoo tattoo too voodoo
woo yoo-hoo

-oo rhymes with some *-ew* words
askew blew brew chew corkscrew crew dew drew
few flew grew interview knew mew nephew new
pew phew screw shrew sinew skew slew threw view

-oo also rhymes with *-ue*
argue avenue barbecue blue clue continue cue due
flue fondue glue hue queue revue rue statue subdue
sue tissue true value venue

Other words that rhyme with *zoo*
canoe   do   ewe   flu   gnu   guru
Hindu   kung fu   menu   Peru
rendezvous   shoe   through
to   tutu   two   you

There was an old man from Peru
Who dreamed he was eating his shoe
He woke in the night
In a terrible fright
And found it was perfectly true.

a
b
c
d
e
f
g
h
i
j
k
l
m
n
o
p
q
r
s
t
u
v
w
x
y
z

Write your own poetry

Limericks

A limerick is a five-line verse which follows a set pattern. It was first made famous by the poet Edward Lear (1812-88). You can find examples of limericks on pages 58 (**There was once a boy called Bill**), 117 (**A young man who came from Japan**) and 129 (**There was an old man from Peru**).

In a limerick
- lines 1 and 2 are longer lines that end with a rhyme
- lines 3 and 4 are shorter lines that end with a rhyme
- line 5 is a longer line that rhymes with lines 1 and 2

Can you complete these limericks?

There was a young schoolboy called Flynn
Who sat on a drawing pin
He leapt up in the air...

You can find words with the rhyming sound *-in* listed under the entry for **win** on page 122, and words with the rhyming sound *-air* under the entry for **air** on page 8.

A daring young girl from Dundee...

You can find words with the rhyming sound *-ee* listed under the entry for **tree** on page 112.

A wizard's apprentice called Matt...

You can find words with the rhyming sound *-at* listed under the entry for **hat** on page 49.

Now see if you can make up a limerick on your own. Try to think of a funny punchline to end it.

Nonsense nursery rhymes

Nonsense nursery rhymes are comical versions of traditional nursery rhymes. For example:

> Mary had a little cow.
> She fed it safety pins
> And every time she milked the cow
> The milk came out in tins.

Here are the first lines of some nonsense nursery rhymes.
Can you complete them?

- ▸ Mary had a little cat.
  She dressed it in a skirt...

- ▸ Little Miss Kettle
  Sat on a nettle...

- ▸ Humpty Dumpty sat on the sofa
  Watching cartoons on TV...

- ▸ Billy, my brother, and I fell out
  And what do you think it was all about?

- ▸ Little Tom Tarpet sat on the carpet
  Licking a big ice cream...

- ▸ Dr Lester went to Chester...

- ▸ Little Bo-Peep can't get to sleep...

- ▸ Monday's child has a goofy grin...

Counting rhymes

A counting rhyme is a rhyme which includes counting.
Some rhymes count up to ten, others count backwards from
10 down to 1.

Can you complete these counting rhymes?

One, Two

One, two
A bath full of glue

Three, four....

Ten Naughty Dragons

Ten naughty dragons blowing smoke-rings in a line,
One set himself on fire, then there were nine.

Nine naughty dragons....

Animal Counting Rhyme

One for the goat in a winter coat.
Two for the ants in striped underpants,
Three for the...

Ten Young Children

Ten young children
 Playing in the park.
The first one said,
 "Pretend I'm a shark."
The second one said,
 "I'm a dinosaur."
The third one said...

Rhyming riddles

The poems on this page are rhyming riddles. Can you solve them?

1

I can spin. I can roll. I can fly through the air.
I go where you hit me. Then I lie waiting there.
I am usually round – sometimes big, sometimes small.
I can make my way over or back from a wall.

2

My first is in ghoul and also in charm.
My second is in magic and twice in alarm.
My third is in cauldron but isn't in fire.
My fourth is in gremlin but not in vampire.
My fifth is in skeleton and in bones.
My sixth is in werewolf but isn't in groans.
My seventh is in spell but not in broomstick.
My eighth's found in treat, but not found in trick.
My ninth is in phantom but isn't in fear.
My whole is the scariest night of the year.

3

Hold it steady in your hand,
Then you will see another land,
Where right is left, and left is right,
And no sound stirs by day or night;
When you look in, yourself you'll see,
Yet in that place you cannot be.

Here is a riddle about an animal with the rhyming words missing. Can you work out what the words are and what the animal is?

> I scratch the leaves that have fallen ___ .
> I am hard to see as my spines are ____ .
> I use the strong claws upon my ___
> To search for insects and slugs to ___ .
> Soon I'll curl in a ball in my ___
> And go to sleep for my winter ____ .

Make up a rhyming riddle of you own. Either choose a subject yourself or write a riddle about an animal or an object, such as a pen, a book or a bicycle.

Epitaphs

An epitaph is a verse written about a person or animal who has died. It is often put on their gravestone. Here are some examples:

> Here lies the body
> Of Percy Thistle
> A ref who's blown
> His final whistle.

> Here lies a teacher Mr Lee
> Who said, "You'll be the death of me!"
> And sitting at his desk one day
> He gave a sigh and passed away.

> In loving memory of Rover
> Who ran out in the road
> And got run over.

Answers: down brown feet eat nest rest (hedgehog)

Here lies Charlotte Cul-de-sac,
A most annoying friend,
She used to drive me round the bend
Until she came to a dead end.

Can you complete these epitaphs?

▸ Here lie the remains of Auntie Vi
  Who strapped on wings and tried to fly...

▸ In memory of Billy Green
  Who took off in a time machine...

▸ Here lies what's left of Mr Bloor...

▸ Here lies a careless boy called Jake...

▸ In memory of fearless Fred...

▸ In memory of little Red Riding Hood...

Can you write some epitaphs of your own?

You could write about a person or an animal – either
real or imaginary. For example, you could write about a
nursery rhyme character, such as Old King Cole, an
imaginary creature, such as Desmond Dinosaur, or a
person with an unusual name, such as Candy Bar.

Rapping

Rapping is a type of rhyming poetry. A rap is a poem with plenty of rhyming and a very strong rhythm, which is often written to be performed to music.

Can you add some verses to this rap about people and their names?

Clap your hands, tap your feet,
Get the rhythm, get the beat.

My name's Grace. I am just ace.
I have got a smile on my face.

Clap your hands, tap your feet,
Get the rhythm, get the beat.

My name's Nasreen. I'm lean and mean.
I'm a star of the disco scene.

Clap your hands, tap your feet,
Get the rhythm, get the beat...

Can you write a fairground rap?
Here are two lines that you can use to get started:

C'mon everybody, let's go to the fair,
There's plenty of things for us to do there...

You can write a rap about any topic.
Choose your own subject and write a rap about it.
You could use these two lines to start your rap:

Come on everybody, let's hear you clap,
We're going to do the ... rap.

Rhyming couplets

One of the ways poets use rhymes is to write rhyming couplets.
A rhyming couplet is a pair of lines that rhyme. For example:

> We like riding on the double-decker bus,
> Up on the top-deck, that's the place for us!

Can you add some rhyming couplets to this list poem?

In My Magic Box

> In my magic box, I will put
>
> The twang of a guitar
> The silver lining of a star
>
> The juicy ripeness of a peach
> The sunlight shining on a beach...

Here is a cautionary rhyme, written in couplets:

Warning: Too Much TV Can Damage Your Health

> This is the tale of Millie Mee
> Who day and night would watch TV.
> Now both her eyeballs have turned square,
> An aerial's growing in her hair.
> All she can do is watch TV
> For Millie's glued to the settee.
> So switch off now. Don't hesitate.
> Make sure you don't share Millie's fate.

Can you write some more couplets to complete these
cautionary rhymes?

This is the tale of Samuel Sprocket
Who set off in his homemade rocket...

This is the tale of Betty Blair
Who never ever washed her hair...

A cheeky boy called Robert Rung
Was always sticking out his tongue...

Write a cautionary tale of your own, for example about someone who is always picking his nose, or who is always boasting, or about someone who does something silly. Write it in rhyming couplets.

Chants

Many chants, like these traditional ones, are written in rhyming couplets:

Sam, Sam, the Dirty Old Man

Sam, Sam, the dirty old man,
Washed his face in a frying pan.
He combed his hair with a donkey's tail
And scratched his belly with his big toenail.

Teacher, Teacher

Teacher, teacher, please come quick
Jennifer Brown's been terribly sick.

Can you complete these 'Teacher, teacher' chants?

Teacher, teacher, what should I do?...

Teacher, teacher, come and have a look...

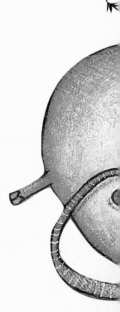

Teacher, teacher, look over there...

Teacher, teacher, help me please...

I Know a Man...

I know a man who wears smelly socks.
I know a man who thinks he's a fox.

Can you complete these 'I know a man' chants?

I know a man with toes on his head...

I know a man whose nose is square...

I know a man who lives in a drain...

I know a man who's the size of a flea...

Homophones

A homophone is one of a group of words which sound
the same but have a different meaning or spelling.
For example, hare and hair are homophones.

Can you find the homophones in these rhymes?

Bare Bear hasn't any hair.
That's why Bare Bear is bare.

Nobody asked her to dance at all,
So she had a good bawl at the ball.

"No, I don't know what to do,"
I said to the man in the queue.
"So I'll take my cue from you."

A gnu who was new to the zoo
Asked another gnu what he should do.
The other gnu said,
Shaking his head,
"If I knew, I'd tell you, I'm new too!"

Rose grows rows of roses.
Each rose Rose grows grows in a row.

Now use this dictionary to find homophones for these words:

beach   board   great   need   pale   pane
pear   read   right   road   sell   sew   sore   stair

Which of the above words has more than one other homophone?

Rhyme patterns

Many poems have four-line verses. A four-line verse is called a quatrain.
Quatrains can have a number of different rhyming patterns.

Pattern 1

In this verse the first and second lines rhyme and the third and fourth
lines rhyme.

As I was going out one day
My head fell off and rolled away.
But when I saw that it was gone,
I picked it up and put it on.

Can you complete the second verse of the poem?

And when I got into the ....
A fellow cried, "Look at your ....!"
I looked at them and sadly .....
"I've left them both asleep in ....!"

Pattern 2

This poem has verses in which the second line rhymes with the fourth line.

> We are the gremlins.
>   We're up to no good.
>   We do things we shouldn't,
>   Not things that we should.
>
> We get up to mischief
>   Of every sort.
> But we're cunning and clever,
> We never get caught.

Can you complete the next verse of the poem?

> We are the gremlins.
> We disconnect wires...

Can you add some more verses in the same pattern describing other things that the gremlins do?

Pattern 3

In this verse the first line rhymes with the third line and the second line rhymes with the fourth line.

> When the night is as cold as stone,
> When lightning severs the sky,
> When your blood is chilled to the bone,
> That's the hour when the witches fly.

Can you complete this verse about a mad magician using the same rhyme pattern?

> In his dark cave the mad magician dwells...

Pattern 4

Sometimes poets write poems in which there is a rhyme within the line. For example:

When Aunty Joan became a phone...

This is known as internal rhyme.

In the following verse the second line rhymes with the fourth line and there are internal rhymes in the first and third lines:

Elastic Jones had rubber bones.
He could bounce up and down like a ball.
When he was six, one of his tricks
Was jumping a ten-foot wall.

Can you complete this verse using the same rhyme pattern:

Ferdinand Fry boasted, "I can fly!"...

Now try to write a poem about a pirate called Peg-Leg Poll in four-line verses, using one of these rhyming patterns.

Index of rhyming sounds

-ab see **crab**
-able see **table**
-ace see **face**
-aced see **paste**
-ack see **back**
-acked see **act**
-act see **act**
-ad see **dad**
-ade see **spade**
-ag see **flag**
-age see **page**
-aid see **spade**
-aight see **gate**
-ail see **tail**
-aim see **name**
-ain see **rain**
-aint see **paint**
-air see **air**
-aire see **air**
-airy see **hairy**
-aist see **paste**
-ait see **gate**
-ake see **lake**
-ale see **tail**
-alk see **talk**
-all see **wall**
-alm see **arm**
-am see **jam**
-ame see **name**
-amp see **stamp**
-an see **van**
-ance see **dance**
-and see **hand**
-ane see **rain**

-ang see **bang**
-ank see **bank**
-anned see **hand**
-ant see **ant**
-ap see **map**
-ape see **grape**
-ar see **car**
-ard see **yard**
-are see **air**
-ark see **dark**
-arm (as in harm) see **arm**
-arm (as in warm) see **storm**
-arred see **yard**
-art (as in start) see **cart**
-art (as in wart) see **sport**
-ary see **hairy**
-ase see **face**
-ash see **crash**
-ask see **ask**
-ass see **glass**
-ast see **last**
-aste see **paste**
-at see **hat**
-atch see **catch**
-ate see **gate**
-aught see **sport**
-aul see **wall**
-ave see **cave**
-aw see **score**
-awk see **talk**
-awl see **wall**

-awn see **corn**
-ay see **X-ray**
-ayed see **spade**
-ayer see **air**

-ea see **tree**
-each see **beach**
-ead (as in head) see **red**
-ead (as in bead) see **weed**
-eak (as in beak) see **speak**
-eak (as in break) see **cake**
-eal see **wheel**
-eam see **dream**
-ean see **queen**
-eap see **keep**
-ear (as in fear) see **ear**
-ear (as in bear) see **air**
-earn see **urn**
-eas see **freeze**
-ease see **freeze**
-east see **east**
-eat (as in heat) see **meat**
-eat (as in sweat) see **jet**
-eck see **neck**
-ed see **red**
-ede see **weed**
-ee see **tree**
-eech see **beach**

-eed see **weed**
-eek see **speak**
-eel see **wheel**
-eem see **dream**
-een see **queen**
-eep see **keep**
-eer see **ear**
-ees see **freeze**
-eet see **meat**
-eeze see **freeze**
-eg see **leg**
-eigh see **X-ray**
-el see **well**
-elf see **elf**
-ell see **well**
-ellow see **yellow**
-elt see **belt**
-en see **hen**
-end see **end**
-ene see **queen**
-ent see **tent**
-ept see **crept**
-er (as in her) see **fur**
-erd see **bird**
-ere (as in here) see **ear**
-ere (as in where) see **air**
-ere (as in were) see **fur**
-ern see **urn**
-erry see **merry**
-ert see **shirt**
-ess see **dress**

-essed see **vest**

-est see **vest**

-et see **jet**

-ete see **meat**

-ette see **jet**

-ettle see **nettle**

-ever see **ever**

-ew (as in chew)
see **zoo**

-ew (as in sew)
see **snow**

-ewed see **food**

-ewn (as in sewn)
see **bone**

-ews (as in sews)
see **nose**

-ews (as in news)
see **use**

-ey (as in key)
see **tree**

-ey (as in they)
see **X-ray**

-ic see **quick**

-ice (as in ice)
see **ice**

-ice (as in practice)
see **kiss**

-ich see **itch**

-ick see **quick**

-ickle see **tickle**

-icks see **mix**

-ics see **mix**

-id see **lid**

-iddle see **middle**

-ide see **ride**

-idge see **bridge**

-ie see **tie**

-ied see **ride**

-ier see **ear**

-ies see **wise**

-iews (as in views)
see **use**

-ig see **big**

-igh see **tie**

-ighs see **wise**

-ight see **light**

-ign see **nine**

-ike see **bike**

-il see **ill**

-ile see **smile**

-ill see **ill**

-im see **swim**

-ime see **time**

-imp see **imp**

-in see **win**

-ind see **find**

-ine (as in
magazine)
see **queen**

-ine (as in fine)
see **nine**

-ing see **king**

-ink see **ink**

-inner see **dinner**

-int see **print**

-ip see **zip**

-ique see **speak**

-ir see **fur**

-ird see **bird**

-ire see **fire**

-irl see **girl**

-irr see **fur**

-irst see **first**

-irt see **shirt**

-ise (as in rise)
see **wise**

-ise (as in promise)
see **kiss**

-ise (as in paradise)
see **ice**

-ish see **fish**

-iss see **kiss**

-issed see **mist**

-ist see **mist**

-it see **hit**

-itch see **itch**

-ite see **light**

-ive see **five**

-iver see **river**

-ix see **mix**

-ize see **wise**

-o (as in slow)
see **snow**

-oad see **road**

-oak see **oak**

-oal see **hole**

-oap see **rope**

-oar see **score**

-oard see **lord**

-oast see **post**

-oat see **coat**

-ob see **job**

-ock see **knock**

-ocks see **fox**

-ode see **road**

-oe see **snow**

-oes see **nose**

-og see **dog**

-ogue see **dog**

-oil see **oil**

-oke see **oak**

-old see **old**

-ole see **hole**

-oll see **hole**

-ome (as in come)
see **mum**

-on (as in son)
see **sun**

-ond see **pond**

-onder see **under**

-one (as in phone)
see **bone**

-one (as in one)
see **sun**

-oney see **honey**

-ong see **song**

-oo see **zoo**

-ood (as in food)
see **food**

-ood (as in blood)
see **mud**

-ood (as in wood)
see **hood**

-ooed see **food**

-ook see **cook**

-ool see **pool**

-ool (as in wool)
see **pull**

-oom see **room**

-oon see **moon**

-oop see **hoop**

-oot see **boot**

-oor see **score**

-ooze see **use**

-op see **shop**

-ope see **rope**

-or see **score**

-ord see **lord**

-ore see **score**

-ored see **lord**

-ork see **talk**

-orm see **storm**

-orn see **corn**

-ort see **sport**

-os (as in radios)
  see **nose**

-ose see **nose**

-oss see **boss**

-ost see **post**

-ot see **pot**

-ote see **coat**

-other see **brother**

-ouble see **bubble**

-ough (as in rough)
  see **puff**

-ough (as in plough)
  see **cow**

-ought see **sport**

-ould see **hood**

-ounce see **bounce**

-ound see **round**

-oup see **hoop**

-our (as in pour)
see **score**

-our (as in hour)
see **tower**

-ous see **us**

-ouse see **house**

-out see **out**

-ove see **love**

-ow (as in now)
  see **cow**

-ow (as in blow)
  see **snow**

-owed see **road**

-owel see **owl**

-ower see **tower**

-owl see **owl**

-own see **town**

-own (as in phone,
  groan) see **bone**

-owned (as
  in crowned)
  see **round**

-ows see **nose**

-ox see **fox**

-oy see **toy**

-oyal see **oil**

-oze see **nose**

-ub see **grub**

-ubble see **bubble**

-uck see **duck**

-ud see **mud**

-ude see **food**

-ue see **zoo**

-ued see **food**

-ues (as in clues)
see **use**

-uff see **puff**

-ug see **jug**

-ul see **pull**

-ule see **pool**

-ull see **pull**

-um see **mum**

-umb see **mum**

-umble see **rumble**

-ume see **room**

-ump see **jump**

-un see **sun**

-unch see **lunch**

-under see **under**

-une see **moon**

-ung see **lung**

-unk see **trunk**

-unny see **honey**

-unt see **hunt**

-up see **up**

-ur see **fur**

-url see **girl**

-urn see **urn**

-urr see **fur**

-urt see **shirt**

-us see **us**

-use see **use**

-ush see **rush**

-uss see **us**

-ust see **dust**

-ut see **hut**

-ute see **boot**

-uy see **tie**

-y see **tie**

-ye see **tie**

-yme see **time**

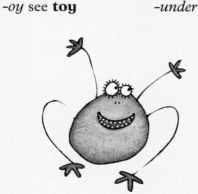

A to Z index

A

aardvark 28
able 106
aboard 69
about 83
above 70
abroad 69
abstract 8
absurd 12
abuse 116
accept 26
accident 108
acclaim 76
accuse 116
ace 34
ache 66
a-choo 128
acorn 22
acrobat 49
across 16
act 8
acute 15
ad 27
add 27
address 30
addressed 118
adept 26
adjust 30
admire 38
admit 49
adore 98
adored 69
adorn 22
advance 27
advert 99
advertise 123
advice 56
advise 123
146

afar 18
afford 69
afloat 20
afraid 101
afternoon 74
again 49, 90
agape 46
age 84
aghast 66
agile 100
ago 100
agog 29
agree 112
agreed 120
agrees 42
aha 18
ahead 91
ahoy 112
aid 101
ail 106
aim 76
air 8
airborne 22
airline 79
airport 103
airy 48
aisle 100
ajar 18
alarm 10
albatross 16
ale 106
alert 99
alibi 110
alike 12
alive 39
all 119
alleyway 124
allow 23
alloy 112

ally 110
almost 86
alone 14
along 101
alphabet 60
although 100
altitude 40
am 60
amen 49
amiss 65
among 70
amp 104
amuse 116
an 117
and 48
announce 16
annoy 112
anorak 13
another 17
ant 10
antelope 96
antique 102
anxious 115
anyway 124
apart 19
ape 46
apologise 123
appeal 122
appear 32
appetite 68
applaud 69
appreciate 45
apricot 87
arcade 101
are 18
argue 128
argued 40

arise 123
aristocrat 49
ark 28
arm 10
armadillo 100
armful 88
around 96
arrayed 101
arrest 118
arrive 39
arrow 100
arrows 80
art 19
ascend 33
ascent 108
ash 24
ashore 98
ask 10
askew 128
asleep 63
astound 96
astride 92
astronaut 103
at 49
ate 45
athlete 72
atmosphere 32
attach 19
attack 13
attend 33
attic 89
attitude 40
attract 8
avenue 128
awake 66
award 69
aware 8

away 124
awful 88
awhile 100
awoke 81

B

baa 18
baboon 74
back 13
backed 8
background 96
backpack 13
backpacked 8
backtracked 8
bad 27
badger 44
bag 39
baguette 60
bail 106
bait 45
bake 616
bale 106
ball 119
ballet 124
balloon 74
bamboo 128
ban 117
band 48
bandit 49
bang 10
bank 11
banned 48
bap 71
bar 18
barbecue 128

barbecued 40
bard 126
bare 8
bareback 13
bark 28
barred 126
barricade 101
base 34
bash 24
basic 89
bask 10
basket 60
bassoon 74
bat 49
batch 19
bawl 119
bay 124
be 112
beach 11
bead 120
beak 102
beam 29
bean 89
bear 8
beast 33
beat 72
beautiful 88
became 76
beck 78
become 75
bed 91
bee 112
beech 11
been 89
beep 63
beer 32
bees 42
beetroot 15

crest *118*
crew *128*
cricket *60*
cried *92*
cries *123*
crime *111*
crimp *59*
croak *81*
crock *65*
crocodile *100*
crocus *115*
crook *21*
croon *74*
crop *99*
croquet *124*
cross *16*
crow *100*
crowed *94*
crown *112*
crowned *96*
crows *80*
crude *40*
crumb *75*
crumble *96*
crunch *70*
crush *97*
crust *30*
cry *110*
cub *47*
cuckoo *128*
cud *75*
cue *128*
cuff *88*
culprit *49*
cup *114*
curious *115*
curl *46*
currant *10*
cursed *39*
curt *99*
cut *55*
cute *15*

cyclist *74*
Czeck *78*

D
dab *23*
dad *27*
daffodil *58*
dairy *48*
dale *106*
dam *60*
damp *104*
dance *27*
dandruff *88*
dank *11*
dare *8*
dark *28*
dart *19*
dash *24*
database *34*
date *45*
dawn *22*
day *124*
daydream *29*
dead *91*
deadpan *117*
deadwood *54*
deal *122*
dealt *12*
dear *32*
debate *45*
debt *60*
decade *101*
decay *124*
decayed *101*
deceased *33*
decide *92*
deck *78*
declare *8*
decorate *45*
deed *120*

deep *63*
deer *32*
defeat *72*
defend *33*
defied *92*
define *79*
degree *112*
degrees *42*
delay *124*
delayed *101*
delete *72*
delight *68*
deliver *93*
den *49*
denied *92*
dent *108*
deny *110*
depart *19*
depend *33*
depress *30*
depressed *118*
descend *33*
descendant *10*
descent *108*
desert *99*
design *79*
desire *38*
despair *8*
dessert *99*
destroy *112*
detach *19*
detail *106*
detest *118*
devote *20*
devour *111*
dew *128*
dial *100*
dice *56*
did *67*
diddle *73*
die *110*

died *92*
dies *123*
dig *12*
digest *118*
digressed *118*
dilute *15*
dim *105*
din *122*
dine *79*
dined *36*
ding *64*
ding-dong *101*
dinner *29*
dinosaur *98*
dip *128*
dire *38*
dirt *99*
disagree *112*
disappear *32*
discard *126*
disco *100*
discotheque *78*
discreet *72*
discuss *115*
disease *42*
disgrace *34*
disgraced *85*
disguise *123*
disgust *30*
dish *39*
dislike *12*
dismiss *65*
dismissed *74*
disobey *124*
display *124*
dispute *15*
dissent *108*
distract *8*
distraught *103*

distress *30*
distressed *118*
ditch *59*
dive *39*
divide *92*
divine *79*
dock *65*
docks *41*
doe *100*
dog *29*
dole *50*
dolphin *122*
domino *100*
dominoes *80*
done *105*
dong *101*
donkey *112*
donkeys *42*
doom *95*
door *98*
dope *96*
dorm *104*
dot *87*
dote *20*
double *17*
doubt *83*
doubtful *88*
dough *100*
doughnut *55*
dove *70*
down *112*
downed *96*
doze *80*
drab *23*
drag *39*
drain *90*
drake *66*
drank *11*
drape *46*
draw *98*
drawer *98*
drawl *119*

drawn *22*
dread *91*
dreadful *88*
dream *29*
dreg *67*
dress *30*
dressed *118*
drew *128*
dried *92*
dries *123*
driftwood *54*
drill *58*
drink *59*
drip *128*
drive *39*
drone *14*
drool *86*
droop *54*
drop *99*
drought *83*
drown *112*
drowned *96*
drug *61*
drum *75*
drunk *113*
dry *110*
dub *47*
dubious *115*
duck *30*
dud *75*
due *128*
duet *60*
duff *88*
dug *61*
dugout *83*
dumb *75*
dump *61*
dune *75*
dung *70*
dungarees *42*
dunk *113*
dust *30*

149

153

peg *67*
pelt *12*
pen *49*
penguin *122*
perform *104*
perfume *95*
perish *39*
permit *49*
persevere *32*
persuade *101*
pert *99*
Peru *129*
pest *118*
pet *60*
petal *78*
petrifies *123*
petrify *110*
pew *128*
phew *128*
Phil *58*
phoenix *74*
phone *14*
photo *100*
piano *100*
pick *89*
pickle *109*
picks *74*
pickup *114*
pie *110*
pier *32*
pies *123*
pig *12*
piggyback *13*
pigsty *110*
pike *12*
pile *100*
pill *58*
pillow *100*
pin *122*
pine *79*
pined *36*

ping *64*
pink *59*
pioneer *32*
pip *128*
pit *49*
pit-a-pat *49*
pitch *59*
pixie *112*
place *34*
placed *85*
plain *90*
plan *117*
plane *90*
plank *11*
planned *48*
plaque *13*
plate *45*
platoon *74*
played *101*
playful *88*
playwright *68*
plea *112*
plead *120*
please *42*
pleat *72*
plight *68*
plop *99*
plot *87*
plough *23*
ploy *112*
pluck *30*
plug *61*
plum *75*
plumb *75*
plume *95*
plump *61*
plunder *114*
plus *115*
plush *97*
pocket *60*
poke *81*
pole *50*

polite *68*
poll *50*
polled *82*
pollute *15*
pond *85*
pong *101*
pool *86*
pop *99*
pope *96*
pore *98*
pork *107*
porridge *16*
port *103*
pose *80*
possess *30*
possessed *118*
post *86*
postcard *126*
postpone *14*
pot *87*
potato *100*
potatoes *80*
pounce *16*
pound *96*
pour *98*
poured *69*
pout *83*
pow *23*
power *111*
pox *41*
practice *65*
pram *60*
prance *27*
prank *11*
pray *124*
prayed *101*
prayer *8*
preach *11*
precious *115*
precise *56*
preen *89*
prefer *44*

preferred *12*
prepare *8*
present *108*
press *30*
pressed *118*
pretend *33*
prevent *108*
prey *124*
preyed *101*
price *56*
prick *89*
prickle *109*
pricks *74*
pride *92*
prim *105*
prime *111*
primp *59*
princess *30*
print *87*
prise *123*
prize *123*
proceed *120*
profile *100*
profound *96*
program *60*
progress *30*
progressed *118*
promise *65*
promote *20*
prone *14*
prong *101*
pronounce *16*
prop *99*
propel *120*
propose *80*
prose *80*
protest *118*
provide *92*
provoke *81*
prowl *83*
prune *75*

pry *110*
pseudonym *105*
pub *47*
puff *88*
puffin *122*
pull *88*
pump *61*
pumpkin *122*
pun *105*
punch *70*
punish *39*
punk *113*
punt *55*
pup *114*
puppet *60*
purr *44*
purred *12*
pursued *40*
pus *115*
putt *55*
pyramid *67*
pyre *38*

Q

quack *13*
quacked *8*
quadruped *91*
quagmire *38*
quail *106*
quaint *85*
quake *66*
quart *103*
quay *112*
queen *89*
quell *120*
quest *118*
queue *128*
queues *116*
quick *89*
quid *67*

quill *58*
quip *128*
quit *49*
quite *68*
quiver *93*
quote *20*

R

rabbit *49*
raccoon *74*
race *34*
raced *85*
rack *13*
radio *100*
radios *80*
radius *115*
rag *39*
rage *84*
raid *101*
rail *106*
railway *124*
rain *90*
rainbow *100*
rake *66*
ram *60*
ramp *104*
rampage *84*
ran *117*
rang *10*
rank *11*
rant *10*
rap *71*
rapid *67*
rare *8*
rash *24*
rat *49*
rat-a-tat-tat *49*
rate *45*
raucous *115*
rave *20*
ravenous *115*

severe *32*
sew *100*
sewn *14*
sews *80*
shack *13*
shade *101*
shadow *100*
shadows *80*
shake *66*
shallow *100*
sham *60*
shame *76*
shampoo *128*
shampooed *40*
shape *46*
shard *126*
share *8*
shark *28*
shave *20*
shawl *119*
she *112*
shear *32*
shed *91*
sheen *89*
sheep *63*
sheer *32*
sheet *72*
shelf *33*
shell *120*
shin *122*
shine *79*
ship *128*
shirt 99
shiver *93*
shoal *50*
shock *65*
shocks *41*
shockwave *20*
shoe *129*
shoelace *34*

shoo *128*
shooed *40*
shook *21*
shoot *15*
shootout *83*
shop 99
shore *98*
shorn *22*
short *103*
shot *87*
should *54*
shout *83*
shove *70*
show *100*
showed *94*
shower *111*
shown *14*
shows *80*
shrank *11*
shred *91*
shrew *128*
shriek *102*
shrill *58*
shrimp *59*
shrine *79*
shrink *59*
shrub *47*
shrug *61*
shrunk *113*
shun *105*
shunt *55*
shush *97*
shut *55*
shy *110*
sick *89*
sickle *109*
side *92*
sigh *110*
sighed *92*
sighs *123*
sight *68*
sign *79*
signed *36*

signpost *86*
sill *58*
sin *122*
sincere *32*
sinew *128*
sing *64*
sink *59*
sinner *29*
sip *128*
sir *44*
sit *49*
site *68*
six *74*
size *123*
skate *45*
skateboard *69*
skew *128*
ski *112*
skid *67*
skies *123*
skill *58*
skim *105*
skimp *59*
skin *122*
skint *87*
skip *128*
skirt *99*
skis *42*
skunk *113*
sky *110*
slab *23*
slack *13*
slam *60*
slang *10*
slap *71*
slapdash *24*
slash *24*
slate *45*
slave *20*
sled *91*
sleek *102*
sleep *63*

sleet *72*
sleigh *124*
slept *26*
slew *128*
slewed *40*
slice *56*
slick *89*
slid *67*
slide *92*
slight *68*
slim *105*
slime *111*
sling *64*
slink *59*
slip *128*
slipper *44*
sliver *93*
slog *29*
sloop *54*
slop *99*
slope *96*
slot *87*
slow *100*
slowed *94*
slows *80*
slug *61*
slum *75*
slump *61*
slung *70*
slunk *113*
slur *44*
slush *97*
sly *110*
smack *13*
smacked *8*
small *119*
smart *19*
smash *24*
smear *32*
smell *120*
smile 100
smoke *81*
smother *17*

smug *61*
snack *13*
snacked *8*
snag *39*
snail *106*
snake *66*
snap *71*
snare *8*
snatch *19*
sneak *102*
sneer *32*
sneeze *42*
snip *128*
snitch *59*
snob *61*
snoop *54*
snooze *116*
snore *98*
snored *69*
snort *103*
snot *87*
snout *83*
snow 100
snowed *94*
snowflake *66*
snows *80*
snub *47*
snuff *88*
snug *61*
so *100*
soak *81*
soap *96*
soar *98*
soared *69*
sob *61*
sock *65*
socks *41*
software *8*
soil *81*
sold *82*
sole *50*
soled *82*
solitaire *8*

solitude *40*
solo *100*
some *75*
someone *105*
son *105*
song 101
soon *74*
sore *98*
sorrow *100*
sort *103*
sought *103*
soul *50*
sound *96*
soundtrack *13*
soup *54*
sour *111*
souvenir *32*
sow *23*
sow *100*
sown *14*
sows *80*
space *34*
spaced *85*
spade 101
Spain *90*
span *117*
spank *11*
spanned *48*
spar *18*
spare *8*
spark *28*
sparred *126*
spat *49*
speak 102
spear *32*
speck *78*
sped *91*
speech *11*
speed *120*
spell *120*
spelt *12*
spend *33*

159